WI
O
C
PENINSULA

Common Animals and Plants

Duncan Butchart

dedicated to Cecil & Shelagh Peterson,
and to all those who strive for the conservation
of the Cape Peninsula

Acknowledgements

Many people have assisted in the compilation of this book and their support is much appreciated. Beth Peterson and Ian Sutherland were a source of great encouragement, and access to their extensive library was invaluable. Penny and Rob Siebert kindly allowed their Cape Town home to become my base on research and photographic trips to the Peninsula, and provided help and advice on my ramblings. I am also grateful to Peter Jenkin for so ably guiding me up, around, and down Table Mountain, on paths he has trod for many years. My wife Tracey assisted with part of the field work, in the reading of various drafts, and in numerous other ways.

Ann Cameron kindly read through the introductory sections and provided useful comments. I am also indebted to specialists who undertook to read and comment upon the drafts of specific sections: Tony Rebelo of the National Botanical Institute at Kirstenbosch, Nicholas Cole and Peter Ross of the Protea Atlas Project, University of Cape Town, and John and Sandie Burrows (plants), Els Dorrat and Peter Linder (restios), Vincent Carruthers (frogs), Paul Skelton and Phil Heemstra of the JLB Smith Institute of Ichthyology, Grahamstown (freshwater and marine fishes respectively), Charles Griffiths of the Department of Zoology, University of Cape Town (marine invertebrates) and Wulf Haacke of the Transvaal Museum (reptiles). Any inaccuracies which may remain are, however, my sole responsibility. Sue Kieswetter of the Avian Demography Unit at the University of Cape Town kindly assisted with the loan of data on bird distribution in the south-western Cape.

The names of the photographers who supplied material additional to my own are listed alongside their respective pictures. I am particularly grateful to Beth Peterson, Lex Hes, Vincent Carruthers, Paul Skelton, Mark Tennant, Nicholas Cole, Ian Sutherland, Peter Lawson, Chris and Tilde Stuart and Debbie Mann for their generous provision of photographs, and to James Marshall for the loan of photographic equipment. I am grateful to Southern Books for initially publishing this book as *Wild About Cape Town*, and to the Natural History team at Struik Publishers for this new edition.

Finally, I dedicate this book to my parents-in-law – Cecil and Shelagh Peterson – for their interest and support, and to all those who are active in the protection of the Cape Peninsula and its wildlife.

Struik Publishers
(a division of New Holland Publishing (South Africa)
(Pty) Ltd)
Cornelis Struik House
80 McKenzie Street
Cape Town, 8001
South Africa
www.struik.co.za

First published in 1996 by Southern Book Publishers
Published in 2001 by Struik Publishers

10 9 8 7 6 5 4 3 2 1

Cover photographs: **Front cover:** Top left, African Penguins (Erhardt Thiel/SIL); Top right, Baboons (Hein von Horsten/SIL); Middle right, Disa Uniflora (Walter Knirr/SIL); Bottom right, Dassie (Shaen Adey/SIL); Bottom left, Cape Sugarbird (Nigel Dennis/SIL) **Back cover:** Top, *Helichrysum vestitum* (Duncan Butchart); Bottom, Spiny Starfish (Duncan Butchart) (SIL = Struik Image Library)

Designed and typeset by Groundhog Graphics, Nelspruit
Reproduced by Hirt & Carter, Cape Town (Pty) Ltd
Printed and bound by NBD, Drukkery Street,
  Goodwood, Western Cape

ISBN: 1 86872 641 X

Contents

INTRODUCTION

Lying at the south-western tip of the African continent, the city of Cape Town is set in a magnificent landscape dominated by Table Mountain and the jagged Peninsula which thrusts into the ocean at Cape Point. Not surprisingly, many of the people living in this wonderful setting are enthusiastic about their surroundings and spend much of their free time close to nature at the seashore or on mountain paths. Cape Town is also a major attraction for visitors who are keen to sample not only its scenery, beaches and fine wine but also, increasingly, the unique plants and animals which are to be found here.

This book has been compiled as a handy, easy-to-use volume which provides a means of identifying and learning about the more common animals and plants, as well as being a starting point for further study. Many books already exist on the identification of South African animals and plants but few of these are regionally specific. Following the pattern of other titles in this series, this book therefore describes only those species which occur on the Cape Peninsula.

From an evolutionary perspective, the flora and fauna of the Cape Peninsula – and the fynbos biome of the south-western Cape as a whole – is of immense interest and importance. The winter-rainfall climate has apparently changed little in the past 70 million years – which is quite exceptional in global terms – and has allowed for remarkable speciation of lifeforms, particularly plants. Isolated from the rest of Africa by physical and climatic barriers, this 'continental cul-de-sac' – as termed by eminent naturalist Jonathan Kingdon – supports an incredible number of endemic species including the Cape Grysbok, Cape Sugarbird, Cape Dwarf Chameleon, Table Mountain Ghost Frog, Cape Kurper, and nearly half of all indigenous plants. These animals and plants are found nowhere else on Earth and their continued survival is dependent upon sensitive land use and the concerted efforts of conservation bodies and the general public.

Regrettably, much of the Cape Peninsula has been irreversibly damaged by man, and some species have become extinct in the process. Modern development began in the 1600's with the arrival of Dutch settlers. These and subsequent colonists from Europe had a major impact on the Peninsula, with the transformation of certain landscapes causing the greatest impact on wild species. Apparently keen to surround themselves with things familiar, early settlers introduced oaks, pines, deer, squirrels and other creatures from their native lands (the populations of some have since exploded in a land where their natural enemies are absent) and felled almost all trees on the once densely-forested eastern slopes of Table Mountain and Hout Bay. In the modern era, urban sprawl, too frequent fires, and pollution are among the major assaults on the environment.

But, despite man's tendency to exploit and develop, the Cape Peninsula still provides a wondrous experience for those interested in nature. The prevalence on mountainsides of shrubby, heath-like plants of the so-called fynbos plant community (see p. 12) will quickly come to the attention, as will the virtual absence of indigenous trees in contrast to the abundance of those from other lands – particularly Australia.

Extensive tracts of land are conserved in three major nature reserves – Cape of Good Hope, Silvermine and Table Mountain – which, at the time of writing, were on the verge of being linked in a single national park. A visit to these areas will reveal a diversity of flowering plants; an abundance of marine invertebrates and fishes; the spectacle of gulls, terns and other seabirds negotiating gusty winds; or chance encounters with troops of baboons. For birdwatchers, the wetlands of Rondevlei, Wildevoëlvlei and Rietvlei provide marvellous opportunities to observe waterbirds, while Kirstenbosch is a haven for all wildlife.

For better or worse, residents of the Cape Town area have unique opportunities to become involved in conservation, with 'hack-outings', river clean-ups, and oil spill rescue operations being among the major issues. By providing a key to the identification of animals and plants, it is hoped that this book will contribute to the growing awareness of nature and complement existing conservation initiatives.

HOW TO USE THIS GUIDE

The habitats

On the following pages, eight distinctive habitats – from rocky shores and mountain slopes to suburban parks and gardens – are identified and their characteristics described. As most animals and plants live in particular places under particular conditions, colour coded habitat symbols appear alongside each species to indicate where a species may be expected, as well as to help confirm the identity between those which look alike but occur in different habitats.

The animals and plants

A cross-section of commonly encountered or easily located animals – from mammals to invertebrates – are depicted and described, as well as a few rarer species of particular interest. In addition, mention is made of less common similar species (ss) with which they might be confused. Birds occupy the largest section as they are of greatest appeal to most people, and are usually fairly easy to observe. All species are arranged in such a way that those with similar characteristics appear together. All alien animals are marked with an asterisk (*).

The section on plants features a mere fraction of the over 2 000 species recorded on the Peninsula. Many of the alien (non-indigenous) species are also featured, not only because they are often abundant and difficult to ignore, but also in the hope that their identification will contribute to the growing desire for their removal. The approach taken with flowering plants has been to identify representatives of a variety of families and genera so that most species can be identified to this level at least. Alien plants are marked with an asterisk (*).

The common names are those used in the authoritative reference books for each particular group, but taking the initiative of ornithological parlance – and in order to standardise terminology – hyphens have been eliminated from all double-barrelled names. The scientific names of trees and other plants are used ahead of common names, as the latter often differ from place to place, and sometimes relate species to families to which they do not belong; the family of each featured plant is given for this reason. Scientific terms have been kept to a minimum but could not be avoided altogether; an abbreviated glossary of these terms is provided on p. 123.

At the beginning of each section introductory notes provide general hints on identification, and other reference books are listed. In addition to this, a detailed list of books for further reading is provided on p. 122.

The photographs

Where possible, photographs have been taken or selected to demonstrate key identification features. Where male and female of one species differ, the sex not illustrated is described in the text. In most cases, plants have been photographed in close-up, to best illustrate leaves, flowers or fruit; for most trees, however, the photograph alone is not always sufficient for identification purposes so reference to the accompanying text is vital. Some difficult-to-photograph birds and other animals have been illustrated with colour paintings.

CAPE PENINSULA

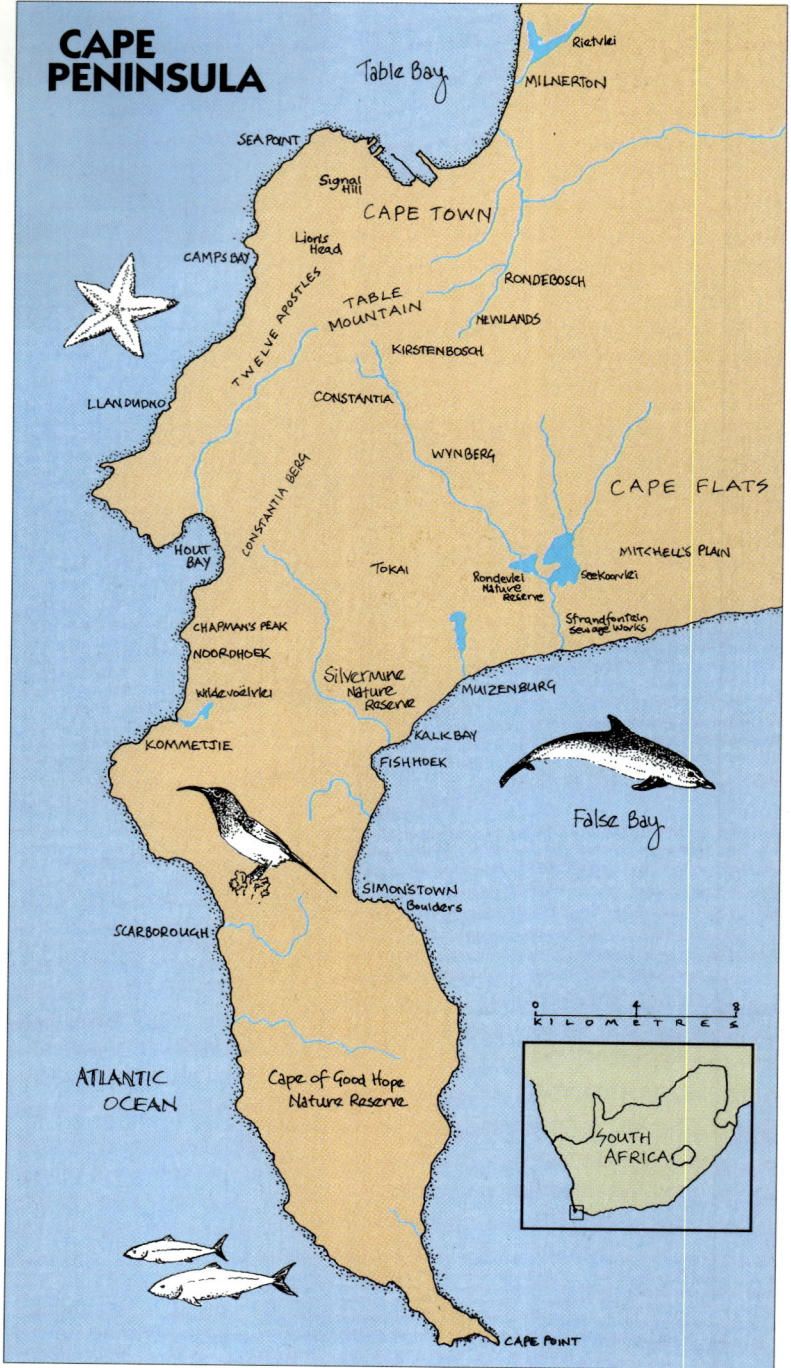

Table Bay

Rietvlei

MILNERTON

SEA POINT

Signal Hill

CAPE TOWN

Lion's Head

CAMPS BAY

RONDEBOSCH

TWELVE APOSTLES

TABLE MOUNTAIN

NEWLANDS

KIRSTENBOSCH

LLANDUDNO

CONSTANTIA

WYNBERG

CAPE FLATS

CONSTANTIA BERG

HOUT BAY

MITCHELL'S PLAIN

TOKAI

Rondevlei Nature Reserve

Zeekoevlei

Strandfontein Sewage Works

CHAPMAN'S PEAK

NOORDHOEK

Silvermine Nature Reserve

MUIZENBURG

WILDEVOËLVLEI

KOMMETJIE

KALK BAY

FISH HOEK

False Bay

SIMON'STOWN
Boulders

SCARBOROUGH

ATLANTIC OCEAN

Cape of Good Hope
Nature Reserve

KILOMETRES

SOUTH AFRICA

CAPE POINT

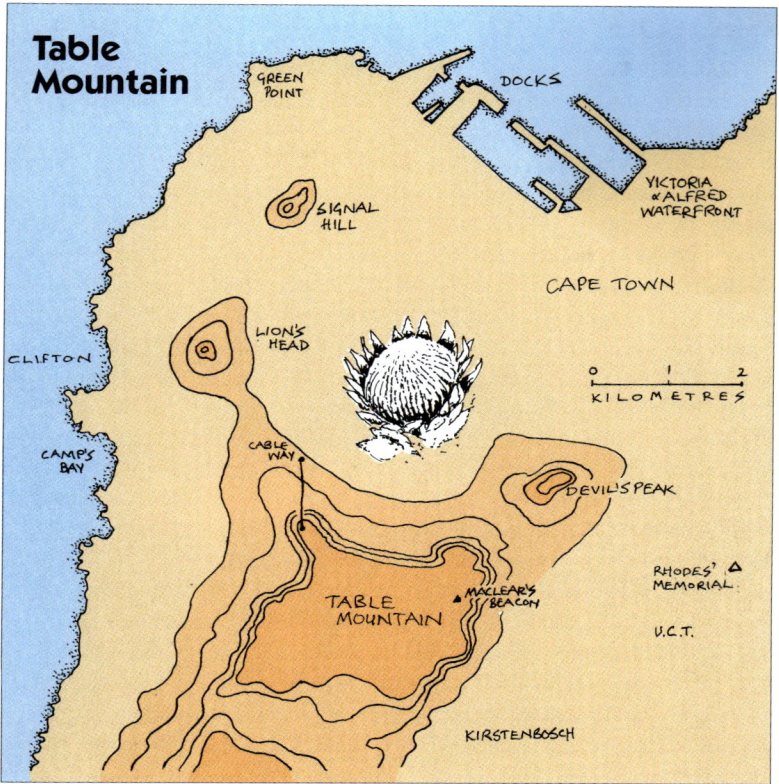

Table Mountain

GREEN POINT

DOCKS

VICTORIA & ALFRED WATERFRONT

SIGNAL HILL

CAPE TOWN

LION'S HEAD

CLIFTON

CAMP'S BAY

CABLE WAY

DEVIL'S PEAK

0 1 2
KILOMETRES

TABLE MOUNTAIN

MACLEAR'S BEACON

RHODES' MEMORIAL

U.C.T.

KIRSTENBOSCH

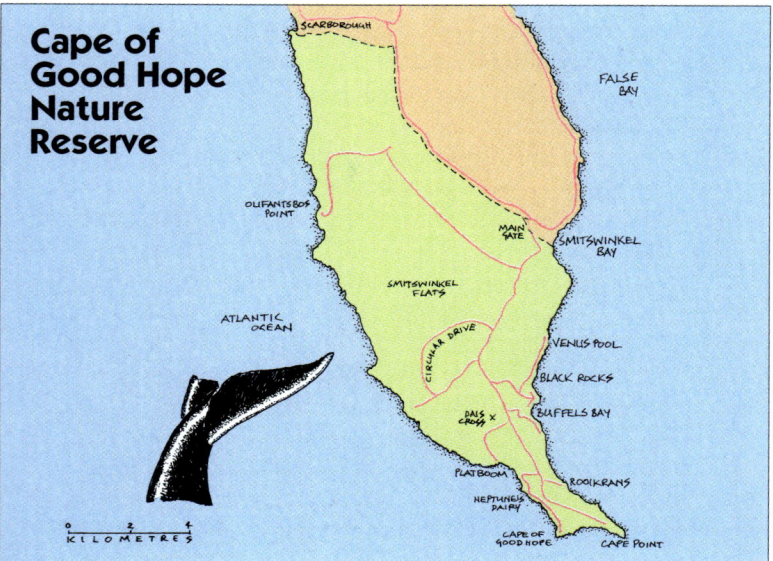

Cape of Good Hope Nature Reserve

SCARBOROUGH

FALSE BAY

OLIFANTSBOS POINT

MAIN GATE

SMITSWINKEL BAY

SMITSWINKEL FLATS

ATLANTIC OCEAN

CIRCULAR DRIVE

VENUS POOL

BLACK ROCKS

BUFFELS BAY

DAIS CROSS ×

PLATBOOM

ROOIKRANS

NEPTUNE'S DAIRY

CAPE OF GOOD HOPE

CAPE POINT

0 2 4
KILOMETRES

7

GEOLOGY AND TOPOGRAPHY

To understand the geology of the Cape Peninsula, an imaginary journey hundreds of millions of years back in time is helpful. 600 million years ago, the flat landmass of what is today the south-western Cape lay beneath the sea off the southern edge of the great continent of Gondwanaland. Volcanic activity at this time then caused it to rise above the ocean, with lava outflows piercing the base and forming rounded granite domes before the whole landscape subsided back to the ocean floor. Layer upon layer of mud and sand were subsequently piled upon this base. Then, an estimated 200 million years ago, great movements within the Earth caused the solidified shelf of sediments to buckle and rise out of the ocean. Most of the landmass was tilted in the process, as is today obvious in the Cape Fold Mountains to the north, but the southernmost part remained horizontal. When Gondwanaland began to split apart some 125 million years ago (giving rise to modern day Africa, South America, India, Australasia and Antarctica), forces of erosion came into play and the plateau was eroded at its sides to leave the flat-topped Table Mountain as a monument of the past.

Today the Peninsula is comprised of three easily distinguished rock types. The lower reaches of the mountains consist primarily of finely textured **Malmesbury Shale** which is fairly soft and weathers easily; Cape Town itself rests on this base. Beneath the shale is **Cape Granite** which protrudes in places as the result of the ancient volcanic activity described above, and is most conspicuous along rocky shorelines such as at Simon's Town on False Bay and below the Twelve Apostles from Sea Point to Llandudno. The dominant rock of the mountains themselves is a combination of sandstone and quartzite known to geologists as **Table Mountain Sandstone**; with its obvious strata, this rock resembles a multi-layered cake with numerous vertical cracks. This quartzitic sandstone is eroded by wind and water to create hollows and oddly shaped rocks characteristic of the summit of Table Mountain and parts of the Cape of Good Hope Nature Reserve. Grey in colour, the sandstone weathers to reddish-brown and is often colonised by various species of lichen.

The erosion process which ate away at the plateau 125 million years ago took away the landmass east of Table Mountain, which was subsequently encroached upon by the ocean to create False Bay. Comparatively recent deposits of windblown sand accumulated on the northern shore of the Bay in what is now known as the Cape Flats.

With this geological history, the Peninsula is a landscape of rugged mountains, sheltered valleys and deeply incised ravines. Numerous streams drain from the mountains, often forming marshes on flat areas, and entering lagoons close to the sea. The shoreline is uneven and jagged, with sandy beaches in bays.

CLIMATE

The Cape Peninsula enjoys a Mediterranean climate characterised by cool wet winters and warm dry summers. This is opposite to the rest of South Africa, which is a summer rainfall region, but the same as places lying at similar latitudes such as Chile and south-western Australia.

The climate is influenced by two main factors, namely the South Atlantic High Pressure System and the icy Benguela Current which sweeps northward from Antarctica. During the summer months, the high pressure system lies south of the Peninsula where it usually prevents cold fronts from crossing onto the mainland. The passing of these cold fronts is followed by strong south-easterly winds which blow across the Peninsula. The more moderate south-easters bring welcome relief to the heat and humidity of summer, but the stronger winds – which may gust at speeds of up to 100 km – send people scurrying for cover and cause trees to bend like grass. Table Mountain's famous 'table cloth' is a result of these winds which pick up moisture from False Bay and push air up and over the mountain where it condenses as cloud. Daytime temperatures in summer average 25 °C, occasionally exceeding 30 °C.

During winter, the high pressure system moves northward, allowing cold fronts to pass across the Peninsula. Strong north-westerly winds then signal the approach of rain which sets in until the cold front moves north or east. Until the next front arrives, still, sunny weather may prevail. Winter temperatures average 19 °C, rarely dropping below 6 °C; frost is almost unheard of near the coast, but snow may fall on Table Mountain.

Although winter and summer climates are well defined, they are not invariable and the weather on the Peninsula is notoriously unpredictable. Icy winds can suddenly interrupt a sub-tropical summer's day, and balmy weather may prompt bathers to visit the beach in midwinter. Rainfall and wind may be extremely localised with storms raging in one place while clear, still weather prevails nearby; Cape Point experiences an average of only 300 mm of rain each year, while the Kirstenbosch area receives about 1 300 mm. Needless to say, anyone venturing outdoors should be prepared for a change in the weather and wear or carry appropriate clothing.

IDENTIFYING AND WATCHING WILDLIFE

Before setting out to explore the Peninsula, it is a good idea to familiarise yourself with the plants and animals which you are likely to see by studying this book. Although there are many splendid drives in the area, it is only by walking that you will come into contact with the majority of wildlife species. A notebook and binoculars are invaluable, while a camera, sketchbook or portable tape-recorder will enable you to document interesting sightings. A telescope mounted on a sturdy tripod will greatly enhance the observation and identification of whales, dolphins, seabirds and shorebirds. Good walking shoes, hat and neutral-coloured clothes are recommended, as is a lightweight raincoat. Weather conditions on Table Mountain are notoriously unpredictable, so be prepared, walk in pairs or groups if possible, and let someone know where you intend going and when you expect to return.

Simply sitting in a well chosen place is one of the best ways to view wildlife. Providing that you remain still and quiet, birds and other animals will often accept you as part of their environment and may go about their business while you watch.

Exploration of rocky shores should coincide with low tide when most of the shoreline is exposed. It is worthwhile to get down to the beach early in the morning, particularly if there has been a storm during the night, as interesting creatures may be found washed ashore. Scuba diving requires training and guidance but allows you to explore deeper waters around reefs and shipwrecks where fascinating invertebrates and fishes abound.

A good way of building up your knowledge and accumulating information is to make lists and notes on the animals and plants you encounter in particular places. Many of nature's secrets are unravelled by amateur naturalists, rather than by biologists, so your own records may be of real value. Consider your field guides as working tools, not sacred tomes, and don't hesitate to make written remarks and notes in them; these may be of value later for the rapid identification of the same or similar species.

By joining natural history societies such as the Cape Bird Club and Botanical Society, you receive regular literature as well as opportunities to learn from other members. Atlas projects which record distributions (proteas and frogs are currently the focus of two such projects – see p. 123) depend upon input from individuals, and provide focal points for nature study.

Learning when and where to find specific animals and plants comes with experience. Whenever approaching wildlife it is important to ensure that you cause the minimum disturbance – not only will this allow you the best possible view but it will also allow animals to behave naturally.

FYNBOS – WHAT IS IT?

The word 'fynbos' is an Afrikaans derivation of the Dutch *fijn bosch*, and is used to describe the fine-leaved bushes which characterise the hillsides and valleys of the south-western Cape.

This winter-rainfall part of the continent has a unique and exceptionally diverse flora which qualify it as one of the world's six floral kingdoms, and it is characterised by **three groups of plants**.

Most abundant are the **heath-like** shrubs typified by the family Ericaceae with over 600 species of *Erica*. Very conspicuous at times are the **proteoids** which include the well-known and often spectacular proteas and pincushions, as well as the less impressive conebushes. Proteas and ericas also occur in other biomes in Africa (such as the highlands of the Drakensberg and the Rift Valley), but the third group characteristic of fynbos is entirely restricted to this biome – the **restios** are reed-like plants with sheath-like leaves often in shades of bronze or copper, which grow in various situations.

Although they hardly fit the description of 'fine-leaved', geophytic plants, with underground storage organs (such as tubers and bulbs) including numerous species of beautiful flowering *Watsonia*, *Ixia*, *Gladiolus* and *Amaryllis* are also typical of fynbos, as is the wide variety of ground orchids. Grasses, so prevalent in many other biomes, are not typical of fynbos (with the exception of Renosterveld), although many deliberately or accidentally introduced species occur today.

The huge diversity of fynbos plants – characterised by **fairly small, hard leaves** and **the ability to withstand or regenerate after fire** – has evolved within the ecological boundaries imposed by soils low in nutrients, winter rainfall and summer fires. Far from being a pitfall, however, fires play a vital role in the maintenance of diversity of the fynbos by burning back old growth and stimulating new growth cycles.

These conditions also prevail in four similar biomes in other parts of the world: the Californian *chaparral*, Australian *kwongan*, Chilean *matorral*, and Mediterranean *maquis* or *macchia*. It is no coincidence that the majority of troublesome invader plants on the Peninsula originate from the winter-rainfall regions of Australia, and that several geophytic and other plants of the Cape fynbos are invasive roadside weeds in Australia.

HABITAT DESCRIPTIONS

Planet Earth can be divided into several broad categories of land type. Geographers refer to these as **vegetation zones**, and they include such well-known types as forest, grassland and desert. Recognising the interrelationship between all life forms, ecologists now prefer to use the word **biome** for these broad definitions so as to embrace all the components. Generally speaking, particular plants and animals are characteristic of, and confined to, a particular biome, but there are notable exceptions, particularly among birds and larger mammals.

A biome is determined by **geology** and **climate** and although mankind may modify or even destroy the landscape, its classification does not change. Within each biome, various factors – such as local rainfall, soil type and aspect – give rise to distinct **habitats**.

The Cape Peninsula falls within the **mountain fynbos biome** which stretches from the Cedarberg to Port Elizabeth. On the following pages eight distinct habitats – from rocky shores and beaches, to mountain slopes and summits – are recognised. The characteristics of each are briefly described and some typical plants and animals mentioned. Man-made gardens and parks are also considered to be a distinct habitat, with their own characteristic species.

The colour-coded symbols at the top of each habitat page are used throughout the species accounts as a means of linking the various animals and plants to their preferred habitat. In some cases, the habitat in which a species is found can be a key to its identification. Likewise, reference to these symbols helps one to predict the animals and plants which might be seen in a particular place.

Key to habitat symbols

M Mountain Slopes and Summits

SF Sandflats and Renosterveld

BD Beaches and Dunes

RS Rocky Shores

O Ocean

WR Wetlands and Rivers

F Forests and Plantations

GP Gardens and Parks

Mountain Slopes and Summits

This habitat dominates the Peninsula, incorporating Table Mountain, Devil's Peak, Lion's Head, Constantiaberg and the chain of mountains south to Cape Point. On many of these slopes and summits the natural fynbos flora is still largely intact although alien vegetation flourishes in many areas.

The density and height of the vegetation on the mountains varies according to aspect, with **east- and south-facing slopes receiving more rain and less sunshine than west- and north-facing slopes**. Typical plants of the moister eastern slopes include the Silver Tree *Leucadendron argenteum* and Mountain Cypress *Widdringtonia nodiflora*, while Tree Pincushion *Leucospermum conocarpodendron* (below the Twelve Apostles) and bulbous plants such as *Watsonia*, *Ixia* and *Gladiolus* are among the common plants on the drier western slopes; distribution also varies according to altitude. The summit of Table Mountain is often a harsh environment where wind influences plant growth – among the typical plants are Blisterbush *Peucedanum galbanum* and China Flower *Adenandra villosa*, with various species of restio forming stands in marshy areas.

Baboons and other larger mammals are more or less restricted to this habitat. Typical fynbos birds include the Cape Sugarbird, Cape Siskin, Cape Rock Thrush and Grassbird, with birds of prey soaring in the regular updraughts and winds. Among the smaller creatures often encountered are the Cape Girdled Lizard and Southern Rock Agama, which bask on exposed rocks. The flowering plants attract an abundance of insects, including butterflies such as the aptly-named Table Mountain Beauty.

Sandflats and Renosterveld

The low-lying, non-mountainous areas of the Cape Peninsula may be divided into three categories identifiable by the terrain and dominant plants. These flat areas were the first to be developed because of the relative ease with which infrastructures could be built, and were also put under pressure by agriculture. In recent years, the windswept Cape Flats have been the site for low-cost township development and squatter settlements which have overwhelmed the natural landscape. Needless to say, several species of plants and animals specifically adapted to these habitats have become endangered or locally extinct.

West Coast Strandveld occurs on deep sand and is dominated by succulent plants and various annuals such as the Cape Daisy *Dimorphotheca pluvialis* which put on a massed flowering show in spring. Other than invasive aliens, trees are absent. Birds include seedeaters and the Whitebacked Mousebird. Patches of Strandveld are to be found in the Cape of Good Hope Nature Reserve, and on a narrow fringe along Table Bay.

Lowland Fynbos occurs on deep sand, often merging with the Strandveld. Dominant plants include the heath-like Wild Rosemary *Eriocephalus africanus*, and the Bokmakierie is one of the typical birds.

West Coast Renosterveld occurs away from the coast on fertile soils derived from Malmesbury Shale. Historically dominated by grass, overgrazing has turned many areas into shrubland. Various geophytic plants and ground orchids are common. The Rondebosch Common represents a fragment of this habitat, of which 97% has been lost to wheat farming and other forms of agriculture in the south-western Cape as a whole. Weavers, bishops and waxbills are typical birds.

Beaches and Dunes

The shores of the Cape Peninsula are primarily rocky but there are extensive stretches of pearly-white beaches, such as at Clifton, Muizenberg and Bloubergstrand (pictured above) which are among the most popular with sunbathers and surfers. The very popularity of these larger beaches renders them less attractive to wildlife, however, so the smaller beaches of sheltered bays, and those within the tranquil Cape of Good Hope Nature Reserve, are generally much more rewarding for naturalists.

Open beaches are favoured by a variety of birds which gather to roost in such exposed places in the knowledge that they might easily detect approaching danger. Terns often congregate at favoured beach sites, while gulls cruise back and forth in search of easy pickings. The tiny Whitefronted Plover may be common on undisturbed beaches. For invertebrates, the constant wave action on beaches limits colonisation, but the specially adapted Finger Ploughshell and White Mussel are characteristic. All manner of dead creatures – from whales and seabirds, to jellyfish and bluebottles – may be washed ashore onto the beaches.

Low dunes abut many beaches but these have been degraded in most places by the alien Redeye Wattle *Acacia cyclops* which smothers indigenous plants. Indigenous dune scrub is still to be found in some places – most notably in the Cape of Good Hope Nature Reserve – where typical plants include White Milkwood *Sideroxylon inerme* and Sea Guarri *Euclea racemosa*. Many dune plants produce berries relished by birds such as Cape Bulbul and Redwinged Starling. Common but rarely seen mammals are the Cape Molerat and Cape Dune Molerat.

15

Rocky Shores

Rocky shores of various designs are a feature of the Cape Peninsula and one of the most fascinating of all wildlife habitats. A few hours spent exploring exposed rocks, pools and crevices at low tide will reveal a variety of colourful and interesting lifeforms.

The distribution of the innumerable species of marine invertebrates found in the area is linked to water temperature and the availability of nutrients (see Ocean – opposite), with many being restricted to one or the other side of the Peninsula.

Rocky shores are exceptionally harsh environments, with the rising and falling tides subjecting the organisms which live there to strong wave action, temporary desiccation, and constant variation of light and temperature. Invertebrates such as mussels and barnacles form colonies, with individuals clinging to rocks, while others such as limpets and whelks are more mobile. Animals may be filter feeders with roving tentacles, grazing herbivores which sweep up algae, cunning predators or scavengers. The area between the levels of high and low tide is known as the **intertidal zone** and is divided into bands of smaller zones in which specific organisms dominate (see p. 86).

Certain rock pools may hold water at low tide when the surrounding rock is exposed; among the more interesting animals to be found here are octopus, cushionstars and sea urchins. In addition to the myriad of marine invertebrates, small, cryptically coloured fish such as the Maned Blenny are commonly encountered in rock pools.

Among the birds which forage on rocky shores are the Black Oystercatcher, which splits apart bivalves with its specially adapted bill, the migratory Turnstone and the Little Egret.

Ocean

The waters surrounding the Cape Peninsula support an extremely rich diversity of marine organisms, with numerous exciting opportunities for the observation and enjoyment of nature.

The prevailing debate as to whether or not the Atlantic and Indian Oceans meet at Cape Point is unlikely to ever resolve itself, as the very concept of a boundary to a constantly moving body of water is indeterminate. What can be said, however, is that the distribution of certain fishes and other creatures is strongly influenced by this landmass, with some species confined to either side of the Peninsula; the division is due not only to water temperature, but also to the availability of nutrients. The chilly Benguela Current sweeps northward from Antarctica to collide with the west coast, while the warmer Agulhas Current moves southward from the east coast to influence sea temperatures as far west as False Bay. The upwelling caused by the Benguela Current brings nutrients to the surface resulting in an abundance of microscopic plant life (phytoplankton) and seaweeds. This vegetable matter is the ecological equivalent of grass in savanna ecosystems with the result that a kaleidoscope of marine herbivores and predators flourish.

Whales, dolphins, seals, penguins, albatrosses, gannets and other birds may be seen from the shore, but seabird watching is best done from a boat (deep-sea fishing craft are ideal) during winter (see p. 123).

A host of beautiful, bizarre and fascinating creatures live beneath the waves and may be observed by scuba-divers. Exploration of reefs and shipwrecks opens up a breathtaking new world to the naturalist, but requires proper training (see p. 123) and a fair investment in terms of equipment.

Wetlands and Rivers

Freshwater habitats on the Cape Peninsula may be divided into four categories: the fast-flowing water of **mountain streams**; the gently moving or still water of **pans**; vegetated **marshes** with little or no open water; and the man-made waterbodies of **reservoirs and dams**. These aquatic habitats support a host of animal and plant species some of which are confined to specific sites and are now at great risk or even extinct. As the Peninsula has been developed, so pans and marshes have been drained and streams canalised; combined with the increasing level of pollution, the future of these freshwater systems is insecure.

A number of streams rise in the mountains to spill into the sea around the Peninsula. On the slopes of Table Mountain, these bubbling brooks – with their characteristic tea-coloured water – are home to species such as the Common River Frog, Cape Galaxias, Black Duck, and Red Disa orchid which grows on moist banks. Lower down, most rivers are badly polluted with eroded banks and infestations of alien plants. The Liesbeeck and other rivers are the subject of ongoing reha-bilitation programmes.

The large, reed-fringed wetlands of Rondevlei, Wildevoëlvlei and Rietvlei – which adjoins Milnerton Lagoon – are the best habitats for freshwater birds in the area. The Cape Flats were once dotted with numerous pans but few of these have survived the rapid urbanisation. Marshes, dominated by reeds, sedges and restios, are at their most extensive in the Cape of Good Hope Nature Reserve where the tiny Arumlily Frog is among the many wetland species to be seen.

Reservoirs and dams are generally unattractive to wildlife although various introduced fish often thrive.

Forests and Plantations

Extensive tracts of indigenous evergreen forest once occurred on the eastern slopes of Table Mountain, on the southern slopes above Hout Bay, and perhaps also in Constantiaberg. The valuable timber in these forests was much sought after by the early settlers, however, and it was not long before all but the most inaccessible ravines were denuded of large trees. Today, true forest is to be found only in a few gorges and ravines on the eastern slopes of Table Mountain, particularly above Kirstenbosch. In years gone by, Real Yellowwood *Podocarpus latifolius* probably dominated the forests but few large specimens remain today. The small patches of forest that still exist are nevertheless extremely interesting and support communities of plants and animals found nowhere else on the Peninsula. Among the distinctive trees are the Red Alder *Cunonia capensis,* Assegaai Tree *Curtisia dentata* and Cape Holly *Ilex mitis*, while creepers, ferns, fungi and lichens abound. Birds include the Cape Batis, Sombre Bulbul and Paradise Flycatcher. The forest edge, which receives more sunlight, supports a distinct plant community with Blossom Tree *Virgilia oroboides* and Wild Peach *Kiggelaria africana* being common.

Non-indigenous trees cover extensive areas, either as stands of alien invaders, or as historical plantings such as at Rhodes' Memorial and Tokai. Pine, oak and gum trees were planted extensively by the settlers and subsequent developers but since their negative effects have been determined, many are the subject of costly eradication programmes. Wildlife is sparse among these trees, but the alien Grey Squirrel and Chaffinch are quite at home, while the indigenous Cape Canary, Rameron Pigeon and Redbreasted Sparrowhawk have adapted well.

Gardens and Parks

Gardens and parks occupy much of the less mountainous terrain of the Peninsula, replacing natural vegetation in most cases. This large-scale development of towns and settlements is, however, the primary reason for the precarious status of many plant and animal species.

Although natural habitats are difficult, if not impossible, to recreate, it is possible to develop a garden favoured by wildlife. The object should be to create a diversity of micro-habitats which will, in turn, attract a diversity of birds and smaller creatures. Plants are obviously the most important component, as they are the basis for food chains – most attract insects which are fed upon by birds, bats, lizards and frogs, as well as affording plenty of enjoyment in their own right. A tangled, bushy thicket in one corner of your garden will provide a refuge for shyer creatures, and some birds may nest there. The growth of indigenous plants is often curtailed by herbivorous insects, but if certain plants cannot survive this feeding pressure it is better to let them die, and replace them with something else, than to resort to pesticides which have a domino effect on food chains. The creation of a small pond or mini-wetland may entice water-loving creatures.

The gardens of properties close to the sea are subjected to harsh winds and only hardy dune plants will flourish. White Milkwood *Sideroxylon inerme* can be grown as focal points in such situations.

Most parks, with their expanses of open lawn, are attractive to birds such as plovers, ibises and swallows, as well as the notorious mound-forming molerats. The wonderful Kirstenbosch Botanical Garden (pictured above) is a haven for wildlife, and can also serve as a guide to planning and deciding what to plant in your own garden.

Mammals

The Cape Peninsula and the fynbos biome as a whole supports relatively few species of larger mammals. Although human settlement and agriculture have contributed to the demise of many species in the region, it is doubtful if 'Big Game' was much in evidence even prior to colonisation and development. Larger herbivores, including the now extinct Quagga (recently proven to be a subspecies of Burchell's Zebra) and Bluebuck, probably occurred in the so-called Renosterveld – the only fynbos habitat dominated by grasses which elsewhere are a vital component of savanna ecosystems in which large grazing animals and predators abound. Lion, African Elephant, Black Rhinoceros and Hippo were nevertheless known to have lived on the Peninsula in the past, with the latter having now been reintroduced to Rondevlei. Other reintroductions include Bontebok and Eland to the Cape of Good Hope Nature Reserve, and Grey Squirrel and Fallow Deer (from Europe) to parks. A fascinating variety of insectivores and rodents may be encountered or looked for, while Chacma Baboon are bold and adventurous at Cape Point and elsewhere.

Marine mammals are well-represented, with whales and dolphins frequently entering the still waters of False Bay, and Cape Fur Seals often feeding in the harbour.

Names used here follow those in the standard reference work – *The Mammals of the Southern African Subregion* by J. Skinner and R. Smithers (Univ. of Pretoria, 1990). Chris and Tilde Stuart's *Field Guide to the Mammals of Southern Africa* (Struik, 1988) is a more portable yet fully comprehensive guide book.

Southern Right Whale

The whale most often seen off the South African coast; females calve in bays in late winter and spring. The **absence of grooves on the throat** and **lack of fin on the back** are diagnostic. Crusty white growths on the head are distinctive. Feeds mostly on tiny crustaceans (krill). As it floats when killed, this was the whale most sought after by whalers and was dubbed the 'right' whale to hunt.

Length: up to 16 m Mass: up to 60 000 kg (male)

Humpback Whale

Similar in size to the Southern Right Whale, but a much less common visitor to the area in midwinter and spring. The streamlined shape, **grooves on the white throat** and **small dorsal fin** distinguish it from the previous species. The pointed head is knobbly and the flippers long and white. Highly vocal when breeding; their underwater sounds are the subject of 'whale song' recordings.

Length: up to 15 m Mass: up to 40 000 kg (male)

21

Common Dolphin

The dolphin most often seen around the Peninsula. Indigo-blue above and white below with **criss-cross stripes on the flanks**. The **snout is long**. May gather in large hunting schools of hundreds, or even thousands, in False Bay. Feeds on smaller shoaling fish such as Sardine, and squid. Playful individuals often launch themselves out of the water. Frequently swims in the bow wave of ships.
Length: up to 2.5 m Mass: up to 150 kg

Dusky Dolphin

Similar in size and habits to the Common Dolphin but less frequent in waters around the Peninsula. Schools may number several hundred. **Favours the cooler west coast**. Best told from the previous species by its **short blunt snout**. The upper back is blue-black and the **flanks are grey with darker or paler streaks**. Feeds mostly on squid and smaller shoaling fish.
Length: 2 m Mass: up to 115 kg

Cape Fur Seal

The only seal commonly seen on the South African coast. Males considerably larger than females with thick powerful necks. The coat becomes sleek and glossy when wet. Gregarious, but feeds singly or in small groups, favouring small shoaling fish. Often comes ashore to rest on rocky shores such as at Cape Point. Breeds in large noisy colonies on islands and along the west coast.
Length: 1.5 to 2.2 m Mass: 190 kg (male); 75 kg (f)

Hippopotamus

Massive aquatic herbivore with an almost hairless body, and tiny ears and eyes. The broad mouth has tusk-like teeth. Keeps to water by day, when only its ears, eyes and nostrils protrude above the surface. Comes onto land after dark to feed on grass. Vocal and potentially dangerous. Four were introduced to Rondevlei Nature Reserve between 1981 and 1983 with the first calf being born in 1984.
Height: 1.5 m Mass: up to 2 000 kg (male)

LEX HES

Small Grey Mongoose

Small mongoose with grizzled grey coat and long bushy tail. The **legs and feet are black**. Occurs singly or in family groups, using regular pathways in a home range. **Active by day**. Most commonly seen mongoose in the Cape Town area; fairly tame at Kirstenbosch. Diet includes insects, small rodents and carrion. Related **Yellow Mongoose** has a white-tipped tail and favours more open habitats.
Length: 55 to 69 cm Mass: up to 1 kg

GP **SF** **M**

Water (Marsh) Mongoose

Large, **shaggy-coated** mongoose found in the vicinity of water. Occurs singly or in pairs, using regular pathways and latrine sites within a linear territory. Feeds on frogs, crabs and fish caught mostly in shallow water. Active mainly at night. **Spoor shows claw marks**. Dark colour and aquatic habits may lead to confusion with the larger, short-coated **Cape Clawless Otter**.
Length: up to 1 m Mass: 3 to 5 kg

WR

Feral Cat *

Highly adaptable carnivore with variable coat colour and pattern. Thousands of stray, escaped and unwanted cats frequent alleys, parking lots and drains in the city centre, docks and suburbs. Most active at night, when rodents, birds and scavenged pickings provide the bulk of the diet. Where they occur in nature reserves and offshore islands, they pose a serious threat to ground-nesting birds.
Length: up to 90 cm Mass: up to 5 kg

F **SF** **M** **GP**

Largespotted Genet

Slim, short-legged carnivore with **spotted coat and long ringed tail**, usually **black tipped**. Spots vary in colour from black to rusty. Strictly nocturnal and most often seen in branches of trees or running across roads. Solitary and territorial. Preys on a wide variety of creatures from insects to nestling birds. The similar **Smallspotted Genet** differs in having a **white-tipped tail** and pure black spots.
Length: 1 m Mass: 2 to 3 kg

GP **F** **M**

M

Chacma Baboon

Large, dog-like primate with shaggy, grey-brown coat and long bare snout. Males larger than females. Babies often ride on mother's back. Lives in troops in rocky areas. The call is a deep booming bark. Feeds on a wide variety of plants and animals, occasionally foraging along the coast at Cape Point. Loses fear of people when fed along roads or at picnic sites, and becomes **potentially dangerous**.
Length: up to 1.6 m (male) Mass: 32 kg (male)

LEX HES

M **SF** **F**

Porcupine

Large nocturnal rodent with **long, black and white quills**. Vegetarian, it is an avid digger, feeding primarily on roots and tubers. Tree bark is also favoured. Days are spent hidden in a burrow or among rocks. Although not often seen, its presence may be detected by characteristic gnaw marks on the trunks of trees, or by discarded quills. When threatened, the quills are raised and rattled.
Length: 75 to 100 cm Mass: 10 to 24 kg

MARK TENNANT/AFRICAN IMAGES

M

Rock Dassie

Compact, short-eared mammal with **no obvious tail**. Active by day, it frequently basks in the sun, particularly in early mornings and on cool winter days. Colonies comprise several family units. Latrines are characterised by white and brown urine streaks on rocks, and spherical pellets. The diet includes grass, leaves and berries. May climb into trees to feed. Calls with a sharp bark.
Length: 50 cm Mass: 4 to 5 kg

MARK TENNANT/AFRICAN IMAGES

GP

Fallow Deer *

Medium-sized deer native to Europe but introduced into the Cape sometime prior to 1869. A feral population now occurs in the oak and pine forests at the foot of Table Mountain; most often seen in Rhodes Park. The coat is **fawn with white spots in summer**; duller **grey-fawn in winter**. Only the males possess antlers which are shed and regrown annually. Feeds on leaves and grass.
Height: 90 cm Mass: 95 kg (male)

Cape Grysbok

Small **stocky** antelope with **brick-red coat flecked with white hairs** and a **dark face**. Only the male possesses the **short straight horns**. Occurs singly or in pairs in thick, scrubby fynbos. Primarily nocturnal but may be active in the early morning or on cool, cloudy days. Feeds on herbs, grass and berries but is regarded as a pest in vineyards as it relishes young grapes.

Length: 75 cm Height: 54 cm Mass: 10 kg

F **SF** **M**

Steenbok

Small **slender** antelope with rufous-red coat. The **large rounded ears** and **long legs** are characteristic. Only the male has a pair of sharply pointed horns. Prefers open areas but retreats to dense cover when disturbed. Forages alone or in pairs, sometimes after dark. Feeds on leaves, grass and fruit; may dig for tubers or roots. Rarely seen outside of the Cape of Good Hope Nature Reserve.

Length: 85 cm Height: 50 cm Mass: 11 kg

SF

Klipspringer

Small **stocky** antelope with **grizzled, grey-brown coat**. The **prominent orbital glands** and **habit of walking and jumping on hoof tips** are diagnostic. Only the male has a pair of short pointed horns. Lives in pairs or small family groups on cliffs and rocky slopes. Once common on Table Mountain, but now so rare that a reintroduction programme is apparently being considered.

Length: 85 cm Height: 60 cm Mass: 13 kg

M

Bontebok

Large antelope with **purple-brown coat contrasting with white lower legs, underbelly and rump**. The white patches on the face are joined. Occur in herds of up to 25 usually accompanied by a dominant male. Feeds mostly on grass. On hot days stands facing sun with head lowered. Historically confined to the area between Bredasdorp and Mossel Bay but introduced to the Cape of Good Hope Nature Reserve.

Height: 90 cm Horns: 38 cm Mass: 62 kg (male)

SF

GP

Grey Squirrel *

Large squirrel **native to North America** but introduced into Cape Town at the turn of the century by Cecil John Rhodes from the feral population in Britain. The long bushy tail and tree climbing habits are characteristic. Occurs singly or in family groups where **exotic pine and oak trees** grow. Feeds mostly on pine seeds and acorns, often coming onto the ground. Young are usually raised in a tree hole.
Length: 50 cm (incl. 22 cm tail) Mass: 600 g

SF   M

Scrub Hare

Long-legged and long-eared mammal which occurs singly or in small parties in open areas. The underbelly is off-white and the back fawn-grey. Mostly nocturnal, it feeds on grasses and herbs. May be flushed by day from its hiding place among low bushes or grass tufts, running off in a zigzag manner. The very similar Cape Hare is not known to occur on the Peninsula.
Length: 54 cm Mass: 2 to 3 kg

NATIONAL PARKS BOARD OF SA

F   GP

Forest Shrew

Tiny, mouse-like insectivore with long, wedge-shaped snout and small eyes. The coat is **dark brown or black**. Voracious predator of worms, crickets and other invertebrates. Forages by night or day among fallen leaves and loose soil. The similarly sized **Reddish-grey Musk Shrew** is paler in colour and favours dryer fynbos; the **Greater Musk Shrew** is fawn in colour and larger (16 cm).
Length: 1.2 cm Tail: 4 cm Mass: 12 to 16 g

C & T STUART

M   F   SF

Hottentot Golden Mole

Small, barrel-shaped insectivore with **no visible eyes, ears or tail**. The silky coat is rusty-brown. The snout and front legs are designed for digging and burrowing underground. Teeth are small and sharp; preys upon worms and other invertebrates. Underground activity leaves behind **raised furrows, rarely mounds**. Occasionally seen above ground. Smaller **Cape Golden Mole** is darker with pale eye spots.
Length: 13 cm Mass: 75 g

Common Molerat

Small rodent with barrel-shaped body, **short tail** and **protruding teeth**. The eyes are tiny and the ears covered in fur. The body is uniform sandy-brown above, but paler below. Feeds on tubers, bulbs and roots, burrowing underground and **pushing up large mounds of soil in the process**; unpopular with gardeners. Rarely observed, but may move above ground at night.
Length: 15 cm Mass: 150 g

F **GP**

Cape Molerat

Small rodent with barrel-shaped body, **short tail** and **protruding teeth**. The eyes are tiny and the ears covered in fur. Feeds on tubers and roots, burrowing underground and pushing up mounds of soil. With its **dark mask and white ear patches** this is the most attractive of the three molerats in the area but is rarely seen. The larger **Cape Dune Molerat** (32 cm) is plain sandy-brown.
Length: 20 cm Mass: 250 g

BD **SF**

Cape Gerbil

Small, long-haired rodent with **large rounded ears and sparsely haired tail** which is the same length as its body. The coat varies in colour from greyish-brown to fawn. Confined to the fynbos biome where it lives in small colonies in areas of sandy soil. Active only after dark, when it emerges to feed on seeds. Often hops on its hind legs. Preyed upon by owls, snakes and small carnivores.
Length: 30 cm (incl. 15 cm tail) Mass: 100 g

SF

Cape Spiny Mouse

Small, reddish-grey mouse with white underparts. Distinguished from all other mice by the **spiny hairs on its back interspersed with longer black hairs**. Restricted in distribution to the fynbos of the Cape where it prefers rocky ter-rain. Nocturnal, but may be active in the early morning or late afternoon. Occurs singly or in small colonies. Seeds and soft shoots of plants are the main food.
Length: 17 cm (incl. 8 cm tail) Mass: 22 g

M

NATIONAL PARKS BOARD OF SA

GP

House Rat *

Large, long-tailed rodent with rounded ears and grey-black coat. Its completely **naked tail** is diagnostic. It lives in close proximity to man, particularly in warehouses and storerooms where untidy nests are made with a variety of odds and ends. Like the House Mouse, this species arrived first at South Africa's ports before spreading inland to major towns. Omnivorous and destructive.
Length: 37 cm (incl. 20 cm tail) Mass: 150 g

NATIONAL PARKS BOARD OF SA

GP

House Mouse *

Small, long-tailed rodent with **large rounded ears** and grey-brown coat. Nocturnal and omnivorous. Dependent upon the dwellings and refuse of humans. Untidy nests are made of paper and other rubbish. Breeds prolifically. Notoriously difficult to trap. Thought to have originated in northern Europe, local populations probably expanded from the Cape Town docks.
Length: 16 cm (incl. 9 cm tail) Mass: 18 g

C & T STUART

SF   M   GP

Striped Mouse

Fairly small, long-tailed rodent with rounded ears and **four distinct stripes running down its back**. Unlike most other mice, it is most active during the day. Only occasionally enters households. Feeds mostly on grass seeds. It may be extremely common and makes up the bulk of the diet of raptors such as the Blackshouldered Kite and Rock Kestrel.
Length: 20 cm (incl. 9 cm tail) Mass: 45 g

C & T STUART

WR

Vlei Rat

Short-tailed rodent with a blunt nose, **dark shaggy coat** and round ears. Occurs in dense vegetation near water. Active during both night and day, making use of runs and tunnels in order to reach feeding sites. Grass roots, reeds and sedges are favoured. Preyed upon by Serval and various raptors. Although visible only when skulls are examined, the upper incisors are deeply grooved.
Length: 24 cm (incl. 9 cm tail) Mass: 120 g

Egyptian Fruit Bat

Large, grey-brown bat with **dog-like face and large eyes** – by far the biggest bat in the Cape Town area. Feeds at night on figs, soft fruit and nectar. Roosts by day in large colonies in caves or old buildings. Presence may be detected by **messy feeding habits**; discarded fruit and droppings accumulate below favoured feeding perches. Occurs throughout Africa but was first recorded, and named, in Egypt.

Length: 15 cm Wingspan: 60 cm Mass: 130 g

Temminck's Hairy Bat

Small bat with **woolly, rusty-red fur** contrasting with dark brown wing membranes. The snout is long and pointed and the eyes small. Emerges after dark to feed on moths and other airborne insects, usually foraging less than five metres above the ground. Roosts by day in caves or other dark places, often in the company of other bat species. Like all insectivorous bats it navigates by echo-location.

Length: 10 cm Wingspan: 28 cm Mass: 11 g

Cape Serotine Bat

Very small, insectivorous bat with a pale brown back and off-white underparts. The **snout is pointed and the ears short**. This is the little bat most often seen flying at dusk in the company of swallows and swifts. Small airborne insects such as mosquitoes and moths are hunted well into the night. By day, it roosts in colonies under the eaves of houses or in tree holes.

Length: 8 cm Wingspan: 23 cm Mass: 6 g

Geoffroy's Horseshoe Bat

Small insectivorous bat with a fawn or ginger body. The ears are large and pointed. The tail membrane has a pointed tip. Roosts in colonies of up to 1 000 or more in caves or man-made structures. The **elaborate 'nose-leaves'** – not unlike a horseshoe in structure – are diagnostic. Emerges from its roost at dusk, hunting small insects throughout the night.

Length: 10 cm Wingspan: 32 cm Mass: 17 g

Birds

In comparison to other parts of South Africa, the Cape Peninsula is not endowed with a great diversity of birds although a high percentage of those that *do* occur here are endemic to the country. Of the 162 species featured in this section, about half are dependent upon freshwater or marine habitats so birdwatching is most rewarding at such places. Rondevlei Nature Reserve and the adjacent Strandfontein Sewage Works support great concentrations of aquatic birds, while gulls, terns and shorebirds may be seen all around the coast. Seabirds occasionally drift close the shore, particularly in winter, but are best seen on boat trips beyond the continental shelf; this group of birds are notoriously difficult to identify and only the most predictably seen species are featured.

Unfortunately, three of the bird species endemic to the fynbos – the Cape Rockjumper, Victorin's Warbler and Protea Canary, which are all much sought-after by birdwatchers – are absent from the Peninsula although they may be seen within an hour's drive to the east. Birds such as the European Starling have been introduced into the Peninsula by man, while others such as the Pied Barbet have extended their range with the spread of invasive alien trees.

Sasol Birds of Southern Africa (Struik, 1993) is the most comprehensive field guide and will help you to identify species not featured here. *Essential Birding: Western South Africa* by Cohen and Spottiswoode (Struik, 2000) provides details of the best birdwatching localities on the Cape Peninsula and information on pelagic birding. A list of other useful publications is given on page 122.

Jackass Penguin

Small, black and white penguin with pink skin above the eyes. Sexes alike but male is larger. Immature is dull grey above with white breast. The name is derived from its call – a nasal, donkey-like bray. Feeds on fish by day, returning to land at dusk. Gregarious. Breeding colony at Boulders, south of Simon's Town, provides superb viewing opportunities. Population is at risk from oil spills.
Length: 60 cm

Eastern White Pelican

Massive white bird with huge bill, long neck and short legs. The bare skin around the eye and the upper bill is pink, the lower bill and pouch bright yellow. In flight, the **black flight feathers** are conspicuous. Fish are the primary food. Favours still water. Most reliably seen at Rondevlei Nature Reserve and Strandfontein where groups gather to rest on sandbanks.
Length: 1.8 m

Shy Albatross

Large albatross with black upper wings and **grey back**. The **underwings are white, edged with a thin black border**. The **bill is pale horn with a yellow tip**. Sexes alike. Immature has grey head and grey bill with black tip. Most common during winter. Contrary to its name, it is not shy but quick to snatch fish and scraps from trawlers. Best observed offshore or from Cape Point.
Length: 98 cm Wingspan: 2.4 m

BRENDAN RYAN

Blackbrowed Albatross

Large albatross with black upper wings and **black back**. The **underwings are white with a broad black band on the leading edge**. The **bill is yellow with an orange tip**. Sexes alike. Immature has grey smudges on the head and throat, and grey bill with a black tip; underwings are black. Most common albatross in the area, flocks congregate around trawlers. May come close to shore in windy weather.
Length: 90 cm Wingspan: 2.3 m

MANFRED REICHARDT

Cape Gannet

Large white seabird with **black flight feathers and tail** and **white back**. The **head is straw-yellow**, and a thin black line runs down the throat. Sexes alike but male larger. Immature mottled grey-brown. Large flocks may assemble at fish shoals. Fish caught in a spectacular plunge-dive. Most follow the 'sardine run' to KwaZulu-Natal in winter. Breeds on offshore islands up the west coast.
Length: 85 cm Wingspan: 1.8 m

Southern Giant Petrel

Large, grey-brown seabird with **whitish head and neck**. The large bill is buffy-olive and the eyes white. Adults alike; a pure white form also occurs. Immature is darker. Flight less graceful than albatross. Most common in winter; it may be seen coursing above waves beyond surf zone, or scavenging on beaches. Feared by other seabirds – it preys upon nestlings and invalids, as well as pups at seal colonies.
Length: 90 cm Wingspan: 2 m

LEX HES

BRENDAN RYAN

Whitechinned Petrel

Medium-sized, blackish-brown seabird with a **variable amount of white on the throat**. Underwings are uniformly dark. The **bill is pale green** with a black patch around the nostrils. Sexes alike. Immature resembles adult. Occurs singly or in small flocks, often around trawlers where they compete with Blackbrowed Albatross. Among the noisiest of scavenging birds. Also feeds on fish, squid and crabs.
Length: 54 cm

Sooty Shearwater

Smallish, sooty-brown seabird with no white on the throat. **Underwings have silvery-grey lining**. The bill is black. Sexes alike. Immature resembles adult. Occurs in great flocks or 'rafts' which ride offshore waves. Often outnumbers Cape Cormorant and Cape Gannet alongside which it feeds on small fish, squid and crustaceans. Most common in winter and spring.
Length: 46 cm

MANFRED REICHARDT

Pintado Petrel

Smallish seabird which distinctive **black and white chequered upper wings and back**, black head and **snow-white underparts**. The underwings are white, bordered in black. Sexes alike. Visits the Cape in spring, when huge flocks often gather around offshore trawlers to pick up offal and scraps amid much jostling and fighting. Active by day and night. Sits rather high on water surface.
Length: 40 cm

LOWVELD BIRD CLUB

Broadbilled Prion

Small, blue-grey seabird with black band on leading edge of wings and across back. The underparts are white. Sexes alike. Immature resembles adult. Visits the Cape in winter. Other similar prions are almost indistinguishable but are rare vagrants to the Cape. Feeds on tiny crustaceans and plankton which are captured by skimming the water surface and siphoned through the bill.
Length: 30 cm ss: Slenderbilled Prion

Subantarctic Skua

Medium-sized, dark brown seabird with **broad wings and short tail**. The base of the primary feathers are white, showing on both the dark upper wings and silvery lower wings. The black bill is strong and hooked. Occurs singly or in pairs, mostly in **winter**. Scavenges from washed-up carrion, offal from trawlers, eggs and nestlings; pirates prey from other seabirds. Catches own fish by surface dipping.
Length: 60 cm ss: Arctic Skua

LEX HES

Kelp Gull

Large gull with **black back and wings with white margin**. The **large yellow bill** has an orange spot on the lower mandible. The head, tail and underparts are white. Sexes alike but males larger. Immature resembles **Subantarctic Skua** but white wing patches absent. Scavenges from humans and dominates other gulls; also preys on eggs and nestlings. Resident; numbers on the increase.
Length: 60 cm

Hartlaub's Gull

Medium-sized gull with **pale grey back and wings**. The eyes are dark brown and the bill maroon-red. The head may be washed in pale grey when breeding. Sexes alike. Immature has brown flecks on upper wings. Gathers around fishing boats and is abundant at the Waterfront. Occurs on beaches, sportsfields, rubbish dumps and around food factories. Large breeding colony exists on Robben Island.
Length: 38 cm ss: Sabine's Gull (summer only)

African Darter

Large, dark brown waterbird with a long neck – often held in an S-bend shape – and a long pointed bill. Breeding adults have a rufous throat edged in white. The wings are held outstretched to dry. Dives for fish, which are speared before being brought to the surface. Often swims with only the neck and head above water, leading to its alternative name of Snakebird.
Length: 80 cm

33

Cape Cormorant

Medium-sized **marine** cormorant with **glossy** black plumage. The **tail is short** and the **eyes blue-green**. Adults have a **bright orange patch of bare skin** at the base of the bill. Sexes alike. Immature brownish. **Large flocks fly in long, single-file 'chains' from roosts to feeding sites**. Feeds on shoaling fish often in the company of Cape Gannet. A breeding colony exists on the cliffs at Cape Point.
Length: 65 cm

Bank Cormorant

Large **marine** cormorant with **dull** black plumage. The **tail is short** and the **eyes golden-brown**. There is **no bare skin** on the face. Breeding birds may have a **white rump**. Tuft of feathers on forehead may form a rounded crest. Sexes alike. Immature birds resemble adults. Feeds in deeper water or among kelp beds and rocks where gobies and rock lobster are among the prey. Breeds throughout year.
Length: 76 cm

Crowned Cormorant

Small **marine** cormorant with **longish tail** and **red eyes** surrounded by bare orange facial skin. Adults have a **short stiff crest which is often held erect**. Immature birds dull brown above, paler brown below. Occurs in small numbers in shallow water where it dives for small fish and crustaceans. Resident; breeds throughout the year in small colonies on the west coast or on offshore islands.
Length: 50 cm

Reed Cormorant

Small **freshwater** cormorant with a **long tail** (compared to other cormorants) and **red eyes**. Immatures have an off-white breast. In common with other cormorants, the feathers are not waterproof and it regularly perches with its wings outstretched so that they may dry. Fish are caught underwater. Breeds colonially in large trees or in reedbeds, often in the company of herons or storks.
Length: 52 cm

BRENDAN RYAN

Whitebreasted Cormorant

Large black cormorant with a **snow-white throat and chest** and **short tail.** The **eyes are green** and there is a patch of bare yellow skin at the base of the bill. Immature is dark brown with buffy-white underparts. Occurs in both **marine and freshwater** habitats. Large fish are the favoured prey and are caught under-water. Bulky stick nests are often built on man-made structures.
Length: 90 cm

Swift Tern

Large tern with grey wings, back and tail, and white underparts. Breeding adults have a **black crown** with a **white fore-head**. The **bill is yellow or yellow-green**. Non-breeding adult has smaller black crown; sometimes absent. Sexes alike. Immature mottled. Occurs in flocks which roost on beaches and at estuaries by day. Small fish are caught after a plunge-dive. Breeds on Robben Island.
Length: 48 cm ss: Caspian Tern (red bill)

Sandwich Tern

Medium-sized tern with pale grey wings and back, and white underparts and tail. Non-breeding **summer visitor** from northern Europe. Out of the breeding season, adults have white forehead and crown and a smudgy black nape. Breeding adults have black cap extend-ing to bill. At all times the **black bill with yellow tip** is diagnostic. Often found in the company of other terns.
Length: 40 cm

Common Tern

Small tern with pale grey wings, back and tail, and white underparts. Non-breeding **summer visitor** from northern Europe; some may overwinter. Out of the breeding season, adults have **black crown, white forehead** and **black bill**. Breeding adults have a black cap extend-ing to red, black-tipped bill. Roosts on piers and beaches. Similar non-breeding **Arctic Tern** has white tail and rump; **Antarctic Tern** has grizzled crown.
Length: 34 cm ss: Arctic Tern; Antarctic Tern

35

WR RS

Little Egret

Small, all-white egret with long neck. The **yellow toes at the ends of dark legs** are diagnostic. Fine white plumes droop from the back of the head and mantle during the breeding season. The **bill is black** at all times. Occurs in and around fresh water or along rocky coast where it captures small fish, frogs and crustaceans. Nests colonially, often in the company of other species.
Length: 65 cm ss: Yellowbilled Egret (black toes)

GP WR

Cattle Egret

Small, all-white egret with **relatively short neck and legs**. When breeding, the crown, mantle and chest are adorned in **buffy plumes**, the bill and legs are coral-pink and the toes black. Non-breeding birds have a yellow bill and olive-brown legs and toes. Gregarious. Feeds mostly on dry land in the company of cattle or other mammals which disturb insect prey. Roosts and breeds in reedbeds or trees.
Length: 54 cm

WR

Grey Heron

Large, pale grey heron with **white head and neck**, long **yellow bill** and **pale legs**. A bold black streak runs above and behind the eyes to form a small crest. In flight, the **underwing is uniform grey**. Immature duller, with grey neck. Usually occurs singly on the fringes of estuaries, rivers and dams where it preys on frogs and fish. Nest is a platform of reeds and sticks, built in a tree or reedbed.
Length: 1 m ss: Purple Heron (90 cm)

RS SF

Blackheaded Heron

Large, dark grey heron with **black head and neck**, long **grey bill** and **black legs**. The **throat is white**. In flight, the **underwing is black and white**. Flies with neck tucked in. Immature is paler with a yellow lower bill. Usually feeds away from water in farmlands, and along roadsides where it catches rodents and large insects. Nests are near water, in overhanging trees or reedbeds.
Length: 95 cm

Blackcrowned Night Heron

Small, short-necked heron. The face and underparts are snow-white and contrast sharply with the black crown and mantle. The wings are slate-grey, and the **eyes bright red**. Young birds are brown on the back with white spots. Nocturnal, but may be seen flying from roosts at dusk. Groups roost in dense trees or reedbeds by day. Feeds on frogs, nestling birds and insects.
Length: 56 cm

JOHN CARLYON

WR

African Spoonbill

Large, all-white waterbird with distinctive, spoon-shaped bill. The **long legs and bare face of adults are pink**. Flies with neck outstretched. The bill is used in a sweeping motion in shallow water to capture small crustaceans and aquatic insects; small fish and frogs may also be taken. Occurs singly or in flocks which fly in V-formation. May nest alongside other species in reedbeds or dead trees.
Length: 90 cm

WR

Greater Flamingo

Slender white bird with extremely long neck and pink legs. The **bill is pale pink with a dark tip** (the smaller Lesser Flamingo has a dark maroon bill). The outspread wings are pink and black and spectacular in flight. Immature birds are dusky white with a pale bill and grey legs. Occurs in small flocks, feeding on aquatic micro fauna in shallows. Most frequent at Rondevlei Nature Reserve.
Length: 1.4 m ss: Lesser Flamingo (1 m)

LEX HES

WR

Sacred Ibis

Slender white ibis with long legs and scythe-shaped bill. The **naked black head and neck** are diagnostic. The flight feathers are tipped in black. Breeding adults have the tail adorned with black plumes. The name refers to its place in Egyptian mythology. Small flocks forage in shallow water for insects and frogs or scavenge at rubbish dumps. Breeds in reedbeds. Flocks fly in V-formation.
Length: 90 cm

SF   WR

37

WR

Glossy Ibis

Slender, chocolate-brown ibis with long legs. During the summer breeding season, the plumage becomes glossy and bronzed. Always found at fresh water, where it occurs singly or in small flocks. It wades in the shallows in search of frogs, crustaceans and aquatic insects. Small platform nests are made in reedbeds. Flocks fly in V-formation to and from roosts.
Length: 70 cm

GP

Hadeda Ibis

Heavy-bodied, short-legged ibis, and one of the noisiest of birds. Plumage is pre-dominantly olive-green, but the **shoulders have a metallic sheen of purple and emerald**. Forages on lawns and sports-fields or beneath shady trees where insects and worms are extracted from the soil or among leaves. Groups fly to and from tree-top roosts at dawn and dusk. A stick nest is built in the canopy of a tree.
Length: 75 cm ss: Hamerkop (55 cm)

WR

Spurwinged Goose

Massive, greenish-black goose with a variable amount of white on the face and underside. Bill and legs are pink. Males are considerably larger than females, with bare red facial skin extending beyond the eyes. Occurs in small flocks which spend the day loafing on mudflats or in shallow water, and fly off to feeding grounds in the evening. Grass and tubers comprise the diet. Nests among reeds.
Length: 1 m

WR   GP

Egyptian Goose

Large, chestnut and fawn goose with a **dark mask** around the eyes. In flight, the black and white wings with emerald-green panels are diagnostic. Occurs in pairs or small groups on floodplains and pans, but may congregate in large flocks. Feeds mostly on grass on dry land after dark. Noisy and aggressive during the breeding season. Breeds in a large tree hole or other cavity.
Length: 70 cm ss: South African Shelduck

Cape Shoveller

Medium-sized duck with long flattened bill. The body is pale grey-brown with a speckled appearance. Males have pale heads, **lemon-yellow eyes** and **bright orange legs and feet**. Females have dark eyes and feet. Males frequently chase females across the water. In flight, the turquoise wings and green wing panels are conspicuous. Often seen in the company of other ducks.
Length: 53 cm

WR

Yellowbilled Duck

Medium-sized duck with a **bright yellow bill** capped with a black patch. The grey-brown back feathers are edged in white to give a scaly appearance. In flight, the **emerald green wing panels**, rimmed in white, are conspicuous. Occurs on small dams and larger expanses of water. Known to hybridise with the alien **Mallard Duck** which has formed feral populations around Cape Town.
Length: 57 cm

WR

African Black Duck

Medium-sized, charcoal-black duck with **back spotted in white**, and **orange legs**. In flight, the **sapphire-blue wing panels** rimmed in white are conspicuous. Unobtrusive, it **prefers the moving water of streams and rivers**. Tubers, seeds and insects are eaten. Shy and wary, it keeps to vegetated banks, but may rest on rocks. Pairs defend territories along streams. The call is a loud 'quack'.
Length: 56 cm

WR

Redbilled Teal

Small duck with dark mottled plumage, **black cap** and **crimson-red bill**. The underparts are pale fawn. In flight, the fawn and white wing panel is conspicuous. Usually swims among vegetation. May gather in large flocks of several hundred. Prefers shallow water and is quick to arrive at flooded grasslands. Food consists of grass seeds, grain and small aquatic creatures.
Length: 48 cm

WR

Cape Teal

Small duck with pale mottled plumage, **coral-pink bill** and **red eyes**. It differs from the darker Redbilled Teal in lacking a black cap. In flight, the white panel with a green band is conspicuous. Prefers stretches of open water and is usually seen in pairs or small family groups. Often associates with other ducks. It may dive below the surface for aquatic insects and bulbs.
Length: 46 cm

Southern Pochard

Small, maroon-brown duck. The male is very dark with a pale, **grey-blue bill** and **bright red eyes**. The female is paler with a white, C-shaped line on the neck, and dark eyes. In flight, the long white wing bar is conspicuous. Usually occurs in pairs or small groups, often in the company of other ducks. May be rare or absent during the winter months. Often reluctant to leave the water.
Length: 50 cm ss: Maccoa Duck (46 cm)

Dabchick (Little Grebe)

Very small, duck-like waterbird. Breeding adults have a **chestnut neck and pale spot at the base of the bill**; non-breeding birds have buff-brown neck. Usually in pairs which repeatedly dive below water to catch small fish, crabs and frogs. May be found on any stretch of open water, but favours dams and pans with fringing vegetation. The call is a rattling trill. Young ride on parent's back.
Length: 20 cm

Blacknecked Grebe

Small, duck-like waterbird. Breeding adults have a black head and neck with fine **golden plumes on the cheeks**. The **eyes are bright red**. Non-breeding birds have white cheeks and throat. Usually in small flocks in shallow water with fringing vegetation or in shallow bays off-shore. Dives below water to catch small fish and crustaceans. Most reliably seen at Wildevoëlvlei, north of Kommetjie.
Length: 28 cm ss: Great Crested Grebe (50 cm)

Redknobbed Coot

Black waterbird with **white bill and frontal shield**, complemented by red eyes and a pair of red 'knobs' on the forehead. It is one of the commonest waterfowl and may congregate in large numbers when not breeding. The nest of reeds is built on open water. Pugnacious and aggressive, waterborne chases between rivals are commonplace. Feeds on aquatic plants.
Length: 44 cm

WR

Moorhen

Black waterbird with **red frontal shield and bill with a yellow tip**. The legs and feet are bright yellow and there is a thin white streak running down each flank. Smaller, and with a lighter build than the previous species with which it often shares the same habitat. When out of the water, the short tail is repeatedly flicked up and down to reveal snow-white under-feathers. Feeds on aquatic plants.
Length: 33 cm

WR

Purple Gallinule

Chicken-sized waterbird with purple and turquoise underparts, and olive back. The stout **bill and frontal shield are coral-pink**. Occurs singly or in pairs in dense swampy habitats, but is secretive. Most often seen in the dry season when it occasionally strides out from cover on its long **pink legs** into shallow water. Feeds on tubers, sedge stems, flowers and sometimes on nestling birds.
Length: 45 cm

WR

Black Crake

Small, jet-black bird with **lime-yellow bill and bright red legs**. Inconspicuous and shy but much less so than other crakes; most common at Rondevlei Nature Reserve. The call is a harsh throaty warble, frequently a duet between a pair. The very long toes allow it to run across floating vegetation. Small aquatic insects are the main food. The nest is hidden amongst reeds.
Length: 21 cm

WR

41

LEX HES

RS **BD**

Black Oystercatcher

Stocky **black wader with coral-red bill, eyes and legs**. Sexes alike but females are larger. Immature duller. Usually seen in pairs. Restricted to coastline where it forages on rocky shores or sandy beaches. Mussels and limpets are levered off rocks with its flattened bill. Eggs are laid on bare sand in midsummer where they are vulnerable to people and dogs. Most common on offshore islands.
Length: 44 cm

WR

Blackwinged Stilt

Slender, black and white wader with **extraordinarily long red legs**, and **thin pointed bill**. Immature has grey smudges on the head. Favours mudflats and shallow water, often feeding in the company of larger storks and herons. Frequently bends over to probe the mud for worms and insect larvae. Prone to seasonal movement depending upon water levels.
Length: 38 cm

WR

Avocet

Slender, black and white wader with long legs and distinctive **upturned bill**. Immature birds are dusky grey on the back. Present throughout the year but prone to seasonal movements depending upon water levels in wetlands. Most reliably seen at Rondevlei. Feeds on tiny aquatic creatures, often in the company of flamingos and migratory waders in its preferred habitat of shallow water.
Length: 43 cm

WR

Ethiopian Snipe

Cryptically-plumaged wader with **short legs** and **extremely long bill**. The body is streaked, barred and spotted in chestnut and fawn, providing superb camouflage amongst reeds and grasses. Seldom seen but not uncommon. Probes deep into mud for worms and insect larvae. At the onset of winter, pairs engage in high-speed courtship flights featuring a drumming sound created by the stiff tail feathers.
Length: 28 cm ss: Painted Snipe

42

Turnstone

Stocky wader with **short black bill** and **orange legs**. Plumage is variable with the back mottled in tan, brown and buff to create a tortoise-shell appearance. Prefers rocky shores but may also forage on beaches or mudflats along estuaries. The name is derived from its habit of over-turning stones in search of crustaceans and insects. Non-breeding **summer visitor**, but some individuals overwinter.
Length: 23 cm

BRENDAN RYAN

RS

Grey Plover

Stocky plover occurring singly or in small groups at coastal estuaries and bays. Non-breeding **summer visitor** with grey and white mottled back, streaked breast and white belly. In flight, the **white underwings with black 'armpits'** are diagnostic. Some assume their breeding plumage – black face and underparts – prior to migrating north in April. Call is a plaintive whistle.
Length: 25 cm

BRENDAN RYAN

RS **BD**

Blacksmith Plover

Black, grey and white plover with dark red eyes. The long legs are grey-black. Occurs in pairs or family groups in open habitats, often near water. Like other plovers, it lays its camouflaged eggs on bare ground, relying on egg and nestling camouflage for protection. When nests are threatened, the parents rise into the air above the intruders, chanting their metallic 'tink-tink' call.
Length: 30 cm

BETH PETERSON/AFRICAN IMAGES

SF **WR**

Crowned Plover

Sandy-brown plover with a white under-belly, and **black and white crown**. The **long legs are red**. Occurs in short grass-land; in pairs when breeding, or flocks during winter. Camouflaged eggs are laid on the ground. In defence of eggs and young adults circle above intruders, dive-bombing and calling loudly; they may feign injury in order to distract predators from their nest.
Length: 30 cm

BETH PETERSON/AFRICAN IMAGES

SF **GP**

Curlew Sandpiper

Small, olive-grey wader with diagnostic **down-curved bill**. The back feathers are pale rimmed and the rump is white. The white eye-stripe is usually conspicuous. Abundant **summer migrant**, often gathering in flocks of several thousand at estuaries; in flight, flocks appear to change colour as the birds bank to show white underparts and darker backs. Some assume chestnut breeding dress in April.
Length: 19 cm ss: Knot (25 cm, straight bill)

Wood Sandpiper

Small, grey-brown wader with fairly long yellow legs and a thin bill. The **dark back is boldly spotted in white** and the white eye-stripe extends to the back of the head. In flight, the **white rump** is conspicuous. Common **summer migrant** occurring singly or in loose aggregations. Favours shallow water of marshes and temporary pools; usually avoids estuaries.
Length: 20 cm

Marsh Sandpiper

Slender, pale-grey wader with very long, grey-green legs and **thin bill**. The back has a scaly appearance. Common **summer migrant** usually found on mudflats and in shallow water. Very restless, this stilt-like bird is constantly on the move as it probes the mud for worms and insect larvae. In flight, the **white rump and back** are conspicuous. Considerably smaller than the similar Greenshank.
Length: 23 cm

Greenshank

Medium-sized, pale-grey wader with long, grey-green legs and **slightly upturned bill** with a grey-green base. The back has a scaly appearance. In flight, the **white rump** is conspicuous. Widespread **summer migrant** to estuaries and inland waters where it probes mud for prey. Usually seen singly or in the company of other waders. When disturbed it flies off with a **sharp 'chew-chew-chew' call**.
Length: 32 cm ss: Bartailed Godwit (pinkish bill)

44

Common Sandpiper

Small, grey-brown wader with fairly short, grey-green legs and thin bill. The **plain brown back** and **white shoulder patch in the shape of an inverted C** are diagnostic. Common **summer migrant** usually found foraging alone on mudflats or temporary pools. When walking, the tail is constantly bobbed up and down. In flight, the long **white wingbars** are conspicuous.
Length: 20 cm

WR

Ruff

Heavy-bodied, grey-brown wader with fairly long legs and a **shortish bill about the same length as the head**. The **legs may be orange or black**. The back has a scaly appearance. Common **summer migrant**, but some may overwinter. Occurs in large flocks on inland mudflats or estuaries. Flocks often take off in unison to whirl around before resettling. Males are considerably larger than females.
Length: 30 cm (male), 24 cm (female)

WR

Little Stint

Tiny, **grey-brown** wader with white underparts and **short straight bill**. Non-breeding **summer migrant**, but some may overwinter. Occurs in flocks on inland waters or on mudflats of estuaries. Restless and quick to take flight when disturbed. Probes mud for insects, worms and small crustaceans. Chestnut breeding plumage may be assumed prior to northerly migration in April.
Length: 14 cm

WR

Sanderling

Small, **pale-grey** wader with white underparts. Comparatively **short bill is slightly down-curved**. Small **dark shoulder patches** are most conspicuous in flight. Non-breeding **summer migrant**. Occurs in small flocks on sandy beaches; most often on the west coast. Birds in flocks **run in unison in clockwork-fashion along beaches, following wave back-wash** to capture small molluscs.
Length: 19 cm

BD

BD

Whitefronted Plover

Tiny, **sandy-fawn** plover with **white collar and underparts**. A dark line runs between the short bill and black eyes. Adults live **in pairs** which establish territories along beaches. Immatures may congregate in groups at estuaries. Often stands in a hunched posture and may remain still to avoid detection. Resident. Camouflaged eggs laid on upper beach among plants or washed-up flotsam.
Length: 18 cm ss: Chestnutbanded Plover

WR

Ringed Plover

Tiny, brown-backed plover with white underparts and **orange legs. Summer visitor.** Non-breeding adult has **blackish forehead, eye-mask and chest bar**, and white throat. Immature is duller with broken chest bar. Some adults assume breeding plumage – black mask, chest bar and collar – prior to their northerly migration in April. Usually seen singly or in the company of other wading birds.
Length: 16 cm

WR   SF

Kittlitz's Plover

Tiny, brown-backed plover with **black forehead stripe passing through eye to nape** and **buff breast**. Immature and non-breeding adult differ from immature Whitefronted Plover in broad eye-stripe extending to pale nape. Occurs in pairs or small groups on inland mudflats or fringes of lagoons and estuaries; never on open beaches. Resident. Camouflaged eggs are laid on bare ground.
Length: 16 cm

WR

Threebanded Plover

Tiny plover with plain brown back contrasting with white underparts, and **red eye-ring**. Its name is something of a misnomer, as there are only **two black chest bands**. Occurs singly or in pairs on mudflats alongside fresh water where it searches busily for small insects and worms. Resident. Camouflaged eggs are laid on bare ground. Often associates with migrant waders during summer.
Length: 18 cm

46

Spotted Dikkop

Cryptically coloured, plover-like bird with **long yellow legs** and very large **yellow eyes**. It lacks the grey wing panel and white wing bar of the next species. Nocturnal; roosts in shade by day. A piercing, flute-like call is uttered after dark. The well-camouflaged eggs are laid on bare ground and they and the young are vigorously defended with an open wing display.
Length: 45 cm

GP **SF**

Water Dikkop

Nocturnal, plover-like bird occurring on the edges of lagoons and rivers. The large yellow eyes and long yellow legs are distinctive. The **streaked upperparts, grey wing panel and white wing bar** distinguish it from the previous species (which is found in dry habitats). Occurs in pairs or small groups. The call is a plaintive whistle made after dark. Feeds on small aquatic creatures.
Length: 40 cm

LEX HES

WR

Cape Francolin

Dark brown francolin with delicately patterned plumage. The bill is greyish on the upper mandible and red below. The **legs are orange-red**. Occurs in pairs or family parties which keep to dense cover for the most part. May become tame when fed or left unmolested; common at Kirstenbosch. The only other francolin in the region is the **Greywing**, which has a ginger head and yellow legs.
Length: 35 cm ss: Greywinged Francolin (33 cm)

M **SF** **GP**

Helmeted Guineafowl

Unmistakable, charcoal-grey bird finely spotted in white. The head is capped with a small horny casque – in the shape of a helmet. Not indigenous to the Peninsula, it was introduced from the eastern Cape at the turn of the century. Most common in open areas, farmlands and on lawns at Kirstenbosch. Feeds on insects and seeds. Eggs are laid on the ground among dense vegetation.
Length: 56 cm

SF **GP**

Blackshouldered Kite

Small, pale grey raptor with snow-white head and underparts and diagnostic **black shoulder patches**. The feet and cere are yellow and the eyes bright red. The immature is blotched in ash-brown and white. Often perches on the highest available point and typically wags its tail. Regularly hovers above prey; Striped Mouse makes up the bulk of its diet. The nest is built in a shrub or tree.
Length: 33 cm

African Marsh Harrier

Brown raptor with streaky plumage and long bare legs. The **forewings are rimmed in white**. The eyes are bright yellow. The immature has an off-white chest bar. Always associated with aquatic habitats, it typically flies low and with deep wing beats above wetlands. Feeds on a variety of water-associated birds, rodents, snakes and frogs. Nests on the ground among reeds or restios.
Length: 45 to 50 cm ss: Black Harrier

Steppe Buzzard

Medium-sized raptor mottled in brown and fawn, with a **smudgy pale bar on the breast**. The cere and legs are yellow. Much variation in plumage occurs. In flight the **dark tips of the feathers** and **pale wing panels** are noticeable. **Summer visitor**. Preys mostly on rodents. The **Forest Buzzard** has a boldly blotched chest, is present all year, and keeps to woods such as those at Tokai.
Length: 45 to 50 cm ss: Forest Buzzard (48 cm)

Jackal Buzzard

Medium-sized raptor with charcoal-grey back and wings. The **tail and breast are chestnut**. The underwings show **white wing panels**. Sexes alike. The immature is mottled rufous on back and front. Often 'hangs' in the air in a stiff breeze. Preys mostly on rodents and reptiles. Much less common than the previous species; most regularly seen on Table Mountain and at Tokai.
Length: 50 cm

C & T STUART

BETH PETERSON/AFRICAN IMAGES

African Goshawk

Medium-sized raptor with slate-grey upperparts and **white underparts finely barred in rufous up to the throat**. The legs and eyes are yellow and the **cere is grey**. The female is considerably larger than the male. Favours indigenous forest patches but may visit well-wooded gardens where it draws attention to itself with its **distinctive 'chip' call**. Birds up to the size of Laughing Dove are its prey.
Length: 36 to 40 cm

GP F

Redbreasted Sparrowhawk

Small raptor with **slate-grey upperparts and rufous breast and underparts**. Like the legs and eyes, the **cere is yellow**. Sexes alike but female larger. Immature is mottled on the back and streaked below. Favours exotic plantations and is thought to have colonised the Peninsula in recent years; may visit well-wooded gardens. Usually only seen as it flies from a perch. Small birds are its prey.
Length: 33 to 40 cm

GP F

Black Sparrowhawk

Medium-sized raptor with **white throat and breast contrasting with black upperparts**. The eyes and bare legs are orange-yellow. Females are considerably larger than males. Immatures are variably streaked in fawn and brown. Powerful predator of birds up to the size of francolin, but mostly takes doves. Like other accipiters (goshawks and sparrowhawks) it is unobtrusive and easily overlooked.
Length: 46 to 58 cm

GP F

Black Eagle

Very large, jet-black raptor, with a distinctive **white cross on its back**. The legs and cere are yellow. Sexes alike, but female is larger. Immature is mottled in brown and fawn. Usually seen in pairs, soaring along cliffs such as on Table Mountain and at Cape Point. The nest is a large stick structure built on a ledge. Feeds almost entirely upon Rock Dassies but will also scavenge.
Length: 75 to 85 cm

BETH PETERSON/AFRICAN IMAGES

M

WR

African Fish Eagle

Large, rust-brown eagle with **snow-white head and chest**. Sexes alike but female is larger. Immature is mottled in brown and white. Most frequently seen at Rondevlei and Wildevoëlvlei. May be located by its evocative 'kyow-kow-kow' call. Pairs often perch within sight of each other in tall trees, swooping down to grasp fish from the water, or to 'pirate' a meal from another bird. Nests in a tall tree.

Length: 63 to 73 cm ss: Osprey (55 to 65 cm)

M   RS

Peregrine Falcon

Medium-sized, slate-grey falcon with **white underparts finely barred in grey**. The **black mask and tear-marks** below the eyes are distinctive. Sexes alike but female is larger. Immature is boldly streaked below. Eggs are laid on a cliff ledge. Said to be the fastest of all birds, it easily reaches speeds of over 150 km per hour in stoops. Preys on birds up to its own size. Most often seen at Cape Point.

Length: 38 cm ss: European Hobby

BETH PETERSON/AFRICAN IMAGES

M

Lanner Falcon

Medium-sized, silvery-grey falcon with **buffy underparts**. The **rust-red crown** and dark hood extending as tear-marks below the eyes are distinctive. Immature is streaked on the chest. Flies extremely fast on pointed wings, catching birds of up to its own size. Breeds in winter, in old stick nests of crows or on the bare ledges of cliffs. **Less common than the Peregrine Falcon on the Peninsula**.

Length: 40 cm

BRENDAN RYAN

M

Rock Kestrel

Small kestrel with **pointed wings** and **chestnut back finely spotted in black**. Sexes alike but male has only a single terminal bar on the grey tail. Immature is duller. Eggs are laid in a hole in a cliff or on the ledge of a tall building. Occurs singly or in pairs. Preys mostly on rodents. Commonly seen on the summit of Table Mountain and in the Cape of Good Hope Nature Reserve.

Length: 35 cm

Spotted Eagle Owl

Large, grey-brown owl with dark blotches on the back and fine barring on the breast. The **ear tufts** are distinctive and the **eyes are bright yellow**. Nocturnal, but occurs in suburbs where it often hunts under lights. Sits on roads, often with dire consequences. Breeds in holes in trees or among rocks. Feeds on a variety of small creatures, including winged termites. The call is a low, deep 'whoooo'.
Length: 45 cm

M GP

Wood Owl

Medium-sized, rufous-brown owl with **dark eyes** set in a pale face; there are **no ear tufts**. The underparts are creamy-white with bold barring. The **bill is pale yellow**. Occurs in pairs in forested kloofs of Table Mountain, well-wooded gardens and plantations. The lovely hooting call may be described as 'who, who, who are you'. Nests in a tree hole. Prey includes rodents and insects.
Length: 35 cm

GP F

Marsh Owl

Dark brown owl with buffy underparts and face, and **black bill**. The eyes are black and the small ear tufts barely noticeable. Nocturnal, but may be active in the late afternoon. Forages by flying low over grasslands, farmlands and wet-lands. If disturbed, it flies in circles above the intruder. Nests on the ground among grass. Call is a harsh croak. Occasional at Rondevlei and other wetlands.
Length: 35 cm

WR

Barn Owl

Pale, ghostly looking owl with **white, heart-shaped face** and underparts. The back and wings are reddish-grey. Nocturnal and seldom seen. Rodents and shrews are the favoured prey, but small birds are also taken. Usually lays its eggs in the ceilings of farm buildings, houses, holes in cliffs, or among the dry leaves of palm trees. The call is an eerie, drawn-out screech.
Length: 32 cm

LEX HES

M F GP

51

Laughing Dove

Small, brick-red and grey dove with pink head and breast speckled in black. Abundant in more open habitats such as gardens and city parks. Like other doves, it is dependent on drinking water. Most often found in pairs; forms flocks at food sources. The call is a series of soft cooing notes, often uttered at midday. Feeds mostly on seeds. The frail twig nest is placed in a bush or man-made structure.
Length: 26 cm

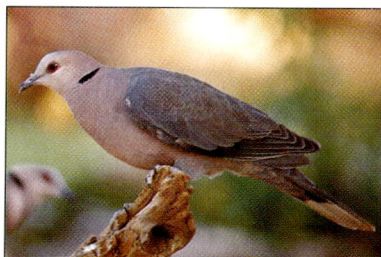

GP **SF**

Redeyed Dove

Large, **pink-headed** dove with bold black neck collar. The breast is rosy-pink and the **red eyes** are surrounded by bare red skin. After the Laughing Dove this is the commonest dove in gardens. Usually rather shy and quick to take flight but often ventures onto lawns. The typical call is a drawn-out 'coooo' but the nasal alarm – **'njeeh'** – is distinctive. Nest and diet is similar to the previous species.
Length: 35 cm

GP **F**

Cape Turtle Dove

Medium-sized, pale grey dove with black neck collar finely edged in white. The **black eyes and pale grey breast** tell it apart from the previous species. The evocative 'kuk-cooo-kuk' call is one of Africa's typical sounds. Usually found in pairs, but may gather in large flocks on agricultural lands or at water. Small twig nest is built within a shrub or tree. Seeds are the main food.
Length: 28 cm

SF **GP**

Rameron Pigeon

Large, dark maroon pigeon with white speckles and spots on the wings and breast. The **bill, bare skin around the eyes, and feet are bright sulphur-yellow**. Occurs in pairs or flocks in well-wooded habitats. Feeds mostly on soft fruit, and is particularly fond of the alien Bugweed *Solanum mauritianum*. May gather in flocks to roost on open branches of large trees in the evening.
Length: 42 cm ss: Cinnamon Dove (26 cm)

F **GP**

Rock Pigeon

Large, reddish-grey pigeon with bold **white spots on the wings**. The under-parts and head are pale grey, and the **eyes are surrounded by bare red skin**. Occurs in pairs when breeding, but flocks may congregate in agricultural lands to feed on fallen grain. May feed alongside other doves in gardens. Usually nests on rocky ledges, but may also breed under the eaves of roofs.
Length: 33 cm

GP **M**

Feral Pigeon *

Large, **variably coloured pigeon** which is predominantly charcoal-grey. Many birds have pale grey backs with dark bands on the wings. Very gregarious, it is most common in the centre of Cape Town where it feeds in the streets, gutters and parks. Also abundant at the Waterfront and docks. Nests are built on the ledges of tall buildings. Descendant of the European Rock Dove.
Length: 33 cm

GP

Redchested Cuckoo

Pale grey bird with long pointed wings. The **chest is rusty-red** and the under-parts buffy with grey bars. Young birds are darker. Elusive **summer migrant**. The repetitive 'piet-my-vrou' call of the male is a familiar sound in midsummer, sometimes carrying on into the night. The female's call is a shrill 'pipi-pipipi'. Lays its eggs in the nests of other birds, particularly the Cape Robin.
Length: 30 cm

GP **F**

Klaas's Cuckoo

Small, emerald-green cuckoo with white underparts and a **small white patch behind each eye**. The male is plain green above and pure white below; the female finely barred with russet. Eggs are laid in the nest of the Cape Batis which then rears the young. Calls 'meitjie-meitjie' from a tree top between July and November. **Diederik Cuckoo** has white on the wings and red eyes in the male.
Length: 18 cm

GP **F**

GP F

Speckled Mousebird

Small, dark grey, mouse-like bird with a very long tail. The underbelly is buffy. The face is black and the **lower bill is white**. Flock members usually fly singly from bush to bush. Individuals huddle together when roosting. Favours tangled growth in which to roost and breed. Berries and soft fruit make up the diet. Call is a harsh chatter. **Commonest mousebird on the Peninsula**.
Length: 35 cm

SF

Whitebacked Mousebird

Small, pale grey, mouse-like bird with a very long tail. The chest is grey, the underparts buffy, and the **feet red**. The **bill is pale with a dark tip**. The **white stripe on the rump is only visible in flight**. Occurs in small flocks with members usually flying one-by-one from bush to bush. Retreats into tangled vegetation when disturbed. Soft fruit and berries are the main food.
Length: 34 cm

BRENDAN RYAN

SF

Redfaced Mousebird

Small, pale grey, mouse-like bird with a long tail. The underparts are buffy. The **bright red facial skin** is diagnostic. Occurs in small flocks which usually fly together from one place to the next. Birds huddle together at their roost. Soft fruit and berries are the main food. A small stick nest is built within a tangled bush. Call is a clear whistle. **Least common mousebird on the Peninsula**.
Length: 34 cm

LEX HES

F M

Fierynecked Nightjar

Nocturnal bird with cryptic, brown and fawn plumage. Rarely seen, and known mostly by its beautiful call – often described as 'good Lord, deliver us'. Most vociferous during the dry season, and particularly on moonlit nights. **Roosts and perches on branches**, seldom alighting on the ground. Moths and other insects are captured on the wing.
Length: 24 cm

Pied Kingfisher

Medium-sized, **black and white** kingfisher with a long black bill. Sexes differ, with the male having a double black bar on the breast, and the female a single broken bar. Occurs in pairs or family groups at water, where it regularly hovers above the surface before plunging in after small fish. May fish from coastal rock pools. Call is a shrill twitter. Eggs are laid in a self-excavated hole in an earth bank.
Length: 28 cm

WR

Giant Kingfisher

Very large kingfisher with **charcoal back flecked in white**. The sexes differ, with the male having only the breast rufous, while the female is rufous on underbelly and underwings. Occurs in pairs or family groups, most often near moving water. Crabs are the favoured prey. The loud 'khak-khak-khak' call is often made while in flight. Eggs are laid in a self-excavated hole in an earth bank.
Length: 46 cm

LEX HES

WR

Malachite Kingfisher

Tiny kingfisher with **bright blue back** and orange-fawn underparts. The long **bill and small feet are scarlet-red**. The crest is malachite-green flecked with black. Sexes are alike but the immature is duller and has a black, not red, bill. Occurs singly or in pairs, keeping to reeds and sedges at the water's edge. Small fish, frogs, tadpoles and aquatic insects are caught. The call is a sharp whistle.
Length: 14 cm

COLIN BELL/WILDERNESS SAFARIS

WR

Burchell's Coucal

Large, **chestnut-red bird with black head** and creamy-white underparts. Flies on broad wings in a floppy, unbalanced manner. In early mornings and evenings, it utters its bubbling call which sounds like liquid being poured from a bottle. Favours wetlands but sometimes ventures onto lawns. Feeds on large insects, rodents and nestling birds. Related to the cuckoos, but it rears its own young.
Length: 44 cm

GP   WR

Whiterumped Swift

Black swift with a **deeply forked tail** often held closed in flight. The **white rump** is conspicuous from above. In common with all swifts, it spends most of its time on the wing, hawking tiny insects, and is physically unable to perch on wires or branches. Compared to swallows, the **wings are long and pointed to create a sickle-shaped outline**. Nests on buildings or cliffs. Absent in midwinter.
Length: 15 cm

Little Swift

Black swift with a **short square tail**, and a white rump. Less prone to flying as close to the ground as the Whiterumped Swift. Very gregarious, often gathering in large flocks to forage and breed. Forms noisy 'circuses' which wheel around breeding colonies. Invariably occurs alongside man, nesting on tall buildings, water towers and concrete bridges. Present all year round.
Length: 14 cm

Black Swift

Medium-sized, all black swift with **no obvious white markings**. The tail is deeply forked. Favours cliffs, such as on Table Mountain, where it breeds in cracks and crevices. Occurs in small flocks which call with a high-pitched scream. May forage over low-lying areas, including the shore, during cloudy weather. Often forages in the company of the Alpine Swift.
Length: 18 cm

Alpine Swift

Large black swift with **white throat and underbelly**; the rump is not white. The tail is deeply forked. Favours cliffs, such as on Table Mountain, where it breeds in cracks and crevices. Small flocks fly at great speed past rockfaces, calling with a shrill scream. May forage over low-lying areas during cloudy weather and regularly feeds in the company of other swifts and swallows.
Length: 22 cm

Greater Striped Swallow

Glossy, royal-blue swallow with off-white underparts lined with **smudgy black streaks**. The **crown and fore-head are dull orange**. A **summer migrant**, it breeds under bridges, culverts and eaves in a closed, mud-pellet nest with a tubular entrance. Often feeds with other swallows. The very similar Lesser Striped Swallow does not occur in the region.
Length: 20 cm

WR · M · GP

European Swallow

Glossy, royal-blue swallow with white belly and underwings. The **throat and forehead are russet**. Immature bird is dusky white and mottled on the throat. Present between late September and April, this is an abundant and familiar **non-breeding migrant** from Europe. Gathers in great numbers to perch on telephone wires each evening at the end of summer. Roosts in reedbeds.
Length: 18 cm

WR · GP

Whitethroated Swallow

Glossy, royal-blue swallow with white underparts divided by a narrow **blue breast band**. The small russet forehead patch is obvious only at close range. An elegant, slow-flying swallow which occurs in pairs or small family groups. Present only in **summer**, it usually builds its nest under low bridges or culverts. Often seen near open water which it skims for insect prey.
Length: 17 cm

GP · WR

Black Sawwing Swallow

All black swallow which differs from swifts in its more languid flight and **absence of any white markings**. The tail is forked. Unlike the swifts it is able to perch on branches. Sexes alike. Usually seen in pairs or family parties. Most active in the late afternoon when it captures air-borne insects on the wing. Eggs are laid in a sandbank burrow. Most reliably seen at Kirstenbosch at the edge of forest.
Length: 15 cm

GP

M

Rock Martin

Plain brown relative of the swallows with **broad wings and a square tail**. Small white spots are visible on the outspread tail. Occurs in the vicinity of rocky outcrops and cliffs, where it builds its nest under overhangs; also breeds on buildings. Smaller **Brownthroated Martin** has pale underbelly and is always found near water; rarer **Banded Martin** is white below with brown chest band.
Length: 15 cm ss: Brownthroated Martin (12 cm)

M

Ground Woodpecker

Large woodpecker with dark brown back and wings flecked with white, grey head and pink wash on the breast. The **red rump** is most noticeable in flight. Sexes alike. Occurs in family parties which forage on the ground in rocky country such as at Cape Point or Table Mountain. Often perches on boulders but shy and difficult to approach. Nest tunnel is excavated in an earth bank.
Length: 25 cm

GP **SF** **M**

Hoopoe

Distinctive, brick-red bird with black and white wings and **fan-shaped crest**. The long curved bill is used for probing the ground for worms and insects. In flight it resembles a giant butterfly. Usually seen singly or in pairs, less often in family groups; occasionally seen on garden lawns. Nests in a cavity in a tree, often quite low to the ground. The call is a repetitive 'hoop-hoop-hoop'.
Length: 28 cm

COLIN BELL

SF **M**

Acacia Pied Barbet

Small, black and white barbet with a diagnostic **scarlet forehead**. A recent immigrant to the Peninsula, having followed the spread of invasive Australian acacia trees in which it excavates its nest hole. Fruit and berries are the main food. The call is a nasal 'nehh-nehh' or a hoopoe-like 'hoop-hoop'. Parasitised by the **Lesser Honeyguide** (opposite) which has also colonised the Peninsula.
Length: 18 cm

Cape Wagtail

Small, grey-brown bird with **long tail**. The underparts are off-white with a thin bar on the throat. True to its name, the tail is constantly bobbed up and down. Confiding and adaptable, it is common around human settlements and also lives in streets and car parks of town centres. Often found near water, including rocky shores. Feeds on insects and is vulnerable to poisoning by garden pesticides.
Length: 19 cm

RS **GP**

Grassveld (Richard's) Pipit

Small brown bird with pale fawn underparts and distinctive, **white outer tail feathers** most obvious in flight. The breast is finely streaked. Much slimmer than the previous species. Occurs in open areas as well as in the vicinity of pans and even on sports fields. The call is a 'chri-chri-chri' whistle, uttered in an aerial display flight. Mostly silent in winter.
Length: 16 cm ss: Plainbacked Pipit (17 cm)

SF

Orangethroated Longclaw

Small, grey-brown bird with **upright stance**. Seen from behind, it appears drab and unremarkable, but the belly and breast are sulphur-yellow and the **throat brilliant orange**. The reason for the exceptionally long claw on the hind toe is unknown. The call is a cat-like 'meauw' and is most often uttered in flight. Occurs in pairs or small family groups, often near water.
Length: 20 cm

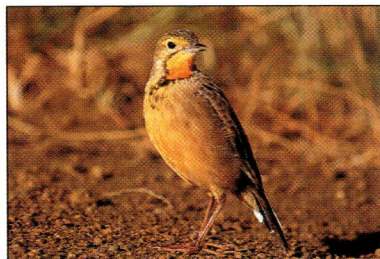

BRENDAN RYAN

M **SF**

Lesser Honeyguide

Small, olive-brown bird with distinctive, **white outer tail feathers**. Lacking any bold colouring and secretive in behaviour, this bird is easy to overlook. In common with other members of its family, it is a brood parasite, laying its eggs in the hole nests of the Pied Barbet (opposite), and is regularly chased by these birds. Feeds on insect larvae and beeswax, but is not known to 'guide' people to honey.
Length: 15 cm

BRENDAN RYAN

SF **M**

59

LEX HES

GP **M** **SF**

Cape Bulbul

Dark brown bulbul with paler under-parts. The **white eye wattles** and **lemon-yellow vent are diagnostic**. Occurs in pairs or family groups in a variety of habitats including thickets of Australian acacias. A confiding resident of gardens. The call is a sharp liquid whistle, or a raspy alarm made when predators are about, or when going to roost. The diet includes fruit and insects.
Length: 21 cm

BRENDAN RYAN

F **GP**

Sombre Bulbul

Drab, olive-brown bulbul with no distin-guishing features other than its **white eyes**. Secretive, it usually keeps to dense cover but may be seen feeding on fruit on exposed branches. Occurs singly or in pairs but is more often heard than seen. The call – described by some as 'Willie – come out and fight – scaaaaared' – is usually uttered from the top of a leafy tree.
Length: 14 cm

LEX HES

GP **F**

Olive Thrush

Olive-brown thrush with distinctive, **orange-yellow bill and legs**. The under-belly has a variable amount of dull orange. The sexes are alike, but the immature is paler and speckled below. Occurs in pairs and is most active at dawn and dusk. Forages on the ground for worms and insects, but also feeds on berries and nestling birds. The call is a flute-like whistle.
Length: 24 cm

M

Familiar Chat

Small, pale brown chat with a **rusty-red tail** most obvious in flight. Its habit of flicking its wings on alighting is an aid to identification. The sexes are alike. Occurs in pairs in open habitats such as on the summit of Table Mountain. Like all chats, it is insectivorous, feeding on small insects and caterpillars taken on the ground. It is often very confiding, and may nest near houses.
Length: 15 cm

60

Cape Robin

Small, grey-brown robin with **orange tail and throat**, and **white eye-stripes**. The sexes are alike, but the immature is buffy and speckled. Occurs in pairs, spending most time on the ground, but retreats quickly to cover if disturbed. May become confiding in gardens. Worms and insects are captured on lawns and among leaf litter. The call is a melodious whistled song or a throaty alarm. Length: 18 cm

LEX HES

F **GP**

Karoo Robin

Small, dark brown robin with **white eye-stripes** and throat and distinctive **white tips to the almost black tail feathers**. Spends most of its time on the ground. The sexes are alike, but the immature is mottled with buff. Very inquisitive, it often makes its presence known by its chattering alarm call. Its song is a jumble of whistles and harsh notes. **Rarely occurs south of the Cape Flats**. Length: 17 cm

SF

Cape Rock Thrush

Small thrush of rocky habitats. The male has a **rust-red back**, orange-ochre underparts and a blue-grey head. The female is paler below with a dusky-brown head. Occurs in pairs, often perching in an upright position on an exposed rock. The call is a clear flutey whistle. The male **Sentinel Rock Thrush** differs in having a **blue grey back**.
Length: 20 cm ss: Sentinel Rock Thrush (19 cm)

BETH PETERSON/AFRICAN IMAGES

M

Stone Chat

Small chat; the male is brown on the back with a **black head, white collar and rufous breast**; the female is paler with a fawn breast. Fences and low bushes are chosen perching places. **Favoured sandveld habitat now reduced by development so much less common than in the past**. Occurs in pairs in rank growth, often near water. Small insects are captured on the ground or in the air. Length: 14 cm

WR **SF**

Grassbird

Small, long-tailed bird with heavily streaked back and rufous head. The **black moustacial streaks** and **ragged end to the tail** are distinctive. Sexes are alike. Occurs singly or in pairs in low scrub, especially among restios, and often near water. Keeps under cover for much of the time so views usually brief; it is conspicuous at Kirstenbosch. Call is a melodious jumble of notes. Feeds mostly on insects.
Length: 20 cm

Karoo Prinia

Tiny, long-tailed bird with dark brown back and pale cream **underparts streaked and blotched in brown**. Sexes alike. Immature is pale yellow below with faint streaks. Occurs in pairs or small parties in fynbos scrub and thickets. Often perches in exposed position, calling repeatedly and holding its tail at a right angle to the body. Call is a sharp 'chleet-chleet-chleet'.
Length: 14 cm

Barthroated Apalis

Tiny, long-tailed bird with grey or dark olive back and pale creamy underparts. The **white eyes**, **white outer-tail feathers** and **black throat collar** are distinctive. Female is paler with thinner collar. Occurs in pairs in evergreen forest or thicket, often entering suburban gardens. Call is a loud 'tilly-tilly-tilly', often a duet between the pair. Feeds on aphids and other small insects.
Length: 13 cm

Knysna Warbler

Tiny, dark brown warbler with **paler throat and underparts.** Extremely shy and secretive, it rarely emerges from cover and is thus rarely seen. Confined to indigenous forest patches and thickets along stream banks on the eastern slopes of Table Mountain between Tokai and Newlands. May be located by following its call – a clear, loud song ending in a rattling trill.
Length: 15 cm

Cape Reed Warbler

Sizeable, pale brown warbler with creamy-white underparts. The **pale eye-stripe** is distinctive. Occurs singly or in pairs in **reedbeds and rank growth** around permanent water. Less shy than other similar warblers which share this habitat. The flutey, robin-like call – 'chirrup-chee-treee' – is more musical than that of other wetland warblers.

Length: 17 cm ss: African Marsh Warbler (13 cm); African Sedge Warbler (17 cm)

WR

Levaillant's Cisticola

Small, **reddish-brown** cisticola with black back feathers edged in brown. The long tail is reddish and **tipped in off-white**. The cap is red-brown. Occurs in pairs or small groups in **rank growth near permanent water**, but avoids dense reedbeds. The call is an insistent 'dswe-dswe-dswe'. More brightly patterned than the Greybacked Cisticola (below) which occurs away from water.

Length: 14 cm

WR

Greybacked Cisticola

Small, **grey-fawn** cisticola with black streaks on the back and dark centres to the wing feathers. The longish **tail is buff-tipped**. The cap is streaked. Occurs in pairs or family groups on hillsides or fynbos **away from water**. Calls include a sharp 'wheee-wheee' alarm or a soft 'pruuut'. Similar **Neddicky** may share the same habitat but has a plain back, shorter tail, and rufous head and wings.

Length: 13 cm ss: Neddicky (11 cm)

BRENDAN RYAN

M

Fantailed Cisticola

Tiny, sandy-brown cisticola with dark streaking on the back and crown. The tail is short, and often held fanned out. Occurs in pairs or groups in **open areas, often near water**. The call is a repetitive 'zit-zit-zit' with a dipping aerial display; it often takes some time to detect the bird in the sky. Outnumbered by the similar **Cloud Cisticola** in the Cape of Good Hope Nature Reserve.

Length: 11 cm ss: Cloud Cisticola (10 cm)

SF

Dusky Flycatcher

Very small, **ashy-brown** flycatcher with **pale eye-stripes** above the dark eyes. The underparts are paler with smudgy streaks and the throat is white. Occurs singly or in pairs in well-wooded habitats; may become tame and confiding. Airborne insects are the prey. The nest is a cup of rootlets and moss placed in a crevice. Similar **Spotted Flycatcher** has a finely streaked crown, and is a summer migrant.
Length: 12 cm ss: Spotted Flycatcher (14 cm)

Paradise Flycatcher

Small, **chestnut-backed** flycatcher with indigo-blue head and smoky-grey under-parts merging to a white vent. The **bill and eye wattles are turquoise-blue**. Breeding male differs from female in extravagant, **ribbon-like tail**. Occurs in pairs in well-wooded places. Tiny, egg-cup nest is often conspicuous at the tip of a branch. Call is a gentle 'wee-we-diddly' or a 'jweet' alarm. **Summer migrant**.
Length: 23 cm (plus 18 cm tail in breeding male)

Cape Batis

Very small, **grey and black** flycatcher with **chestnut wings**. Sexes differ markedly: the male has a broad black breast band and bright yellow eyes; the female has a chestnut throat spot and smudges on the breast, and red eyes. Occurs in pairs in forests on eastern slopes of Table Mountain but may visit gardens. The call is a plaintive 'phooo' or a harsh raspy alarm.
Length: 13 cm

Bokmakierie

Large shrike with olive-green back, grey head and **sulphur-yellow underparts**. The **black gorget** is diagnostic. Sexes are alike. Immature is duller with no gorget. Occurs in pairs in open habitats including rocky hillsides. The repertoire of calls is varied. A loud, ringing duet, beginning 'bok-bok-cheet', probably gives the bird its name. Feeds on beetles and other large insects.
Length: 23 cm

Fiscal Shrike

Black and white shrike with **long tail** and **white V-pattern on the back**. Females have a rust wash on their flanks. Young are mottled and barred in brown and white. Perches conspicuously, in **upright posture**, on fences, wires, walls and outer branches of trees. Feeds mostly on large insects, spearing victims onto thorns or barbed wire – to be retrieved later. Common in open areas.
Length: 23 cm ss: Fiscal Flycatcher (19 cm)

GP SF

Southern Boubou

Black and white shrike with **buffy underparts**. With a **white V-pattern on the back** it is superficially similar to the Fiscal Shrike but the tail is shorter. Female is darker below. Occurs in pairs which keep mostly to the interior of low shrubs and dense foliage. Most common on the eastern slopes of Table Mountain. Strident calls are varied, including liquid or grating notes usually uttered in duet.
Length: 23 cm

GP F

Whitenecked Raven

Large, pitch-black crow with a distinctive **white neck collar**. The massive black bill has a pale tip. Sexes alike but immature is duller. Usually seen in pairs which soar and glide on air currents in rugged country such as around Table Mountain; less common around settlements. Feeds mostly on eggs of other birds and carrion picked up from road; may forage on beaches at low tide. The nest is built on a cliff ledge.
Length: 54 cm

M

Pied Crow

Medium-sized, pitch-black crow with a distinctive **white breast and collar**. The black bill is half the width of the previous species, and the tail slightly longer. Sexes alike but immature is duller. Usually seen in pairs but may gather in larger numbers at food sources. Scavenges on carrion and scraps. Largely absent from mountainous country. It builds its large stick nest in tall trees, or man-made structures.
Length: 50 cm

GP SF

65

BETH PETERSON/AFRICAN IMAGES

GP **M**

Redwinged Starling

Large dark starling with distinctive, **brick-red wings most visible in flight**. The male is glossy blue-black; the female duller with a grey head streaked in black. Occurs in mountainous areas but has adapted well to man's development and is most abundant in the suburbs of Cape Town. Breeds on cliff ledges but also on buildings. Feeds on a wide variety of food. Call is a thin, clear whistle – 'phweeeou'.
Length: 27 cm

SF **GP**

European Starling *

Dark starling with **purple-green plumage covered with buff spots**. Sexes alike. The bill becomes yellow during summer breeding season. Immature dull brown. **Native to Europe**; introduced into Cape Town by Cecil John Rhodes in 1899. Abundant around human habitation but wary of man. Gathers in very large flocks in winter. Breeds under roofs or other structures. Call is a harsh 'cherr'.
Length: 21 cm ss: Wattled Starling (21 cm)

GP **SF** **F**

Cape White-eye

Tiny, green-grey bird with a distinctive **ring of small white feathers around the eyes**. Throat and vent are yellow. Sexes alike. Occurs in pairs during the summer breeding season but forms flocks in winter. Feeds on small insects, such as aphids, as well as on berries and nectar. Often visits gardens; fond of bathing in bird-baths or under sprinklers. The call is a soft, musical warble.
Length: 12 cm

M **GP**

Cape Sugarbird

Large, long-tailed bird endemic to the fynbos biome. Mostly rufous-brown with white moustacial streak and throat, and **yellow vent**. Sexes alike but male has a longer tail. Immature lacks yellow vent. Numbers gather to feed on nectar from flowers belonging to the Proteacea family; seasonally abundant at Kirstenbosch. Sings from an exposed perch. Breeds in winter; cup nest is placed in a bush.
Length: 33 to 44 cm (male), 27 cm (female)

Orangebreasted Sunbird

Small metallic sunbird endemic to the fynbos biome. The male is brilliantly coloured with iridescent green upperparts and head, and **orange underparts**; the **female is uniformly pale olive-fawn**. Occurs in pairs or groups at nectar-rich ericas or *Leonotis*; often in the company of other sunbird species. Breeding peak is in winter; the nest is an oval purse placed on the edge of a bush.
Length: 15 cm (male), 12 cm (female)

GP M

Malachite Sunbird

Large sunbird with sexes not alike. The breeding male is emerald-green with a long tail and yellow 'epaulettes'; when not breeding, he becomes olive-brown with some green patches. Females are pale olive with yellowish, lightly streaked underparts. Occurs in pairs or groups feeding on the nectar of plants such as ericas and proteas. Breeds in winter, the oval nest is built within a dense bush.
Length: 25 cm (male), 15 cm (female)

MANFRED REICHARDT

GP M

Lesser Doublecollared Sunbird

Small metallic sunbird. The male has iridescent green upperparts and head, and a **scarlet breast** bar with blue fringe; the female is **grey-brown, paler below**. Male displays yellow epaulettes in courtship display. Breeds mostly in winter; the nest is an oval purse placed in a bush. Feeds on the nectar of plants such as *Leonotis*, *Salvia*, *Cunonia* and *Erica*. Seasonally abundant at Kirstenbosch.
Length: 12 cm

MANFRED REICHARDT

M SF GP

Red Bishop

Small finch with sexes not alike. The breeding male is **crimson-red with a black face and underbelly**. Females are streaked in fawn and brown with paler underparts and pale eyebrows. Woven nests are hung between reed stems; colonies form in reedbeds. In winter, males assume the drab plumage of the females and large nomadic flocks often feed away from water.
Length: 14 cm

SF WR GP

BETH PETERSON/AFRICAN IMAGES

WR GP

Cape Weaver

Sizeable weaver with **long pointed bill**. The sexes are not alike. Breeding male is golden-yellow with **ginger forehead and throat**. Females are pale olive on the back and creamy-yellow below. Both sexes have **pale eyes**. Insects, seeds and nectar make up the diet. Woven nests are built among reeds or suspended from branches often overhanging water. Call is a swizzling buzz.
Length: 17 cm

WR GP

Masked Weaver

Small weaver with **short pointed bill**. The breeding male is sulphur-yellow with a **black mask** and **red eye**. The female is pale olive on the back and creamy-yellow below. Seeds make up the bulk of the diet. Woven nests are usually hung over water. Call is a swizzling buzz. Has spread onto the Peninsula from the Karoo during the past fifty years but is less common than the Cape Weaver.
Length: 15 cm

BRENDAN RYAN

M WR

Yellowrumped Widow

Medium-sized finch with distinctive breeding plumage. In summer, the male is **pitch-black with sulphur-yellow shoulders and rump** which is puffed out during the courtship display flight. Female is drab and sparrow-like. Non-breeding male loses black plumage to resemble female, but retains yellow shoulders. Occurs in small groups in mountain wetlands and restio patches.
Length: 15 cm

LEX HES

WR GP

Pintailed Whydah

Tiny finch. Male in breeding dress is black and white with an extremely long, ribbon-like tail of black feathers. The **pink bill** is retained by the non-breeding male which resembles the drab, sparrow-like female. In summer, the male is usually accompanied by harem of up to six females. Eggs are laid in the nest of the **Common Waxbill**. Favours open habitats, often near water.
Length: 12 cm (plus 22 cm tail in breeding male)

Cape Sparrow

Small, **chestnut-backed** sparrow with white underparts. The male has a black and white face. The female is paler overall with a grey and white face. Occurs in pairs during the summer breeding season. The untidy straw nests are built in bushes or on buildings. Flocks may form in winter. Feeds on seeds and scraps. Familiar bird in gardens, and also in city parks and on streets.
Length: 15 cm

SF GP

House Sparrow *

Small, grey-brown sparrow with a streaked back. The male has a **grey crown and rump**, white cheeks and black throat. The female has no distinguishing features other than a thin pale eye-stripe. An **alien species** dependent upon man, it occurs in pairs or small groups around buildings and other man-made structures. Abundant on city streets, in gardens and at the docks.
Length: 14 cm

GP

Cape Bunting

Small finch with distinctive, **black and white facial stripes**. The head and mantle is grey, the wings chestnut and the throat and breast pale putty. Sexes alike. Immature is duller with paler wings. Occurs in pairs or small flocks in hilly areas with exposed rocks. May feed and breed on the shoreline. Seeds and small invertebrates make up the diet. The nest is a cup of grass placed low in a bush.
Length: 16 cm

RS SF M

Chaffinch *

Small finch **native to Europe** but introduced into the Peninsula by Cecil John Rhodes at the end of the last century; occurs nowhere else in South Africa. Male has pink face and underparts with blue-grey head; female much paler. Most often seen in the pine forests of Tokai and Newlands but also at Hout Bay; may visit well-wooded gardens. Males sing from an exposed perch in spring.
Length: 14 cm

GP F

Cape Canary

Small canary with olive-yellow back, yellow underparts and **grey back of head**. Male is more brightly coloured than the female. Immature is duller with streaks on the breast. Occurs in pairs or small flocks which feed on seeds and grasses, usually on the ground. Sings beautifully, with a typical canary warble uttered from a high perch. Favours exotic pine trees in which to nest and roost.
Length: 13 cm

GP M F

Bully Canary

Small thickset canary with a **massive bill**. The back and head is olive-yellow, and the undersides pale yellow. The **broad yellow eye-stripes** are distinctive. Usually seen singly or in pairs. Males sing from a favoured song post but rarely stay in one area for long. Feeds on seeds, including those of alien acacias and pines. The brighter **Yellow Canary** is largely confined to flat country.
Length: 15 cm ss: Yellow Canary (13 cm)

M SF

Cape Siskin

Small finch with olive-brown back and pale yellow underparts. Male is more brightly coloured than the female. Immature is boldly streaked on the head and breast. The **tail feathers are white-tipped**. Occurs in pairs or small flocks which search quietly for seeds under bushes and trees. Found only in the fynbos of the southern Cape; most reliably seen at Kirstenbosch and near Cape Point.
Length: 12 cm

M

Common Waxbill

Tiny, pale grey finch with rosy under-parts and long tail. The **bill and eye-mask are bright pink**. The whole body is finely barred. Sexes alike. Immature birds are paler, with a black bill. Occurs in small flocks in rank growth in the vicinity of water, especially in stands of restios; often in the company of other seed-eaters. Feeds mostly on ripening grass seeds.
Length: 13 cm

WR

Reptiles

The Cape Peninsula supports a fairly diverse range of reptiles, with over twenty species of snake; about twenty lizard species including two geckos and one chameleon; one terrapin and four tortoises. The huge Leatherback Turtle occurs offshore but is rarely seen. Of the reptiles found here a large number are endemic to the southern African sub-region but surprisingly few (apart from three of the four tortoises) are restricted to the fynbos biome. Eighteen of the more commonly encountered reptiles are featured in this section.

Reptiles are generally shy and most species retreat in the face of development. For this reason, areas with natural vegetation support greater numbers and a greater diversity of species. Most are usually encountered by chance, although certain species are restricted to particular habitats and may be actively searched for in such places. The majority of lizards favour rocky or open areas and are active by day, while geckos forage on walls or tree bark after dark. Tortoises and terrapins are active by day but most snakes are nocturnal and therefore seldom seen. Nine venomous species occur – five potentially lethal – but they will usually only bite in defence, and then as a last resort. If confronted by a snake, the best strategy is to remain calm and allow it every possible avenue of escape; any attempt to catch or kill it will only increase your chances of being bitten. No lizards are poisonous.

The names used in this section follow those in the *Field Guide to the Snakes and Other Reptiles of Southern Africa* by Bill Branch (Struik, 1988) – the most comprehensive and compact reference book for the region.

Angulate Tortoise

Medium-sized tortoise with the shell finely ridged and often boldly patterned in black and fawn but becoming uniformly sandy-fawn with age; it is neither hinged nor serrated on its rim. The male has a **horn-like projection** on the lower shell below its throat which is used in combat. Feeds on grasses and flowers. Eggs are laid in a burrow after rain. Population is much reduced due to housing on Cape Flats.
Length: 20 cm ss: Parrotbeaked Tortoise (8 cm)

SF

Leopard Tortoise

Large tortoise with a dull, dome-shaped shell which is neither hinged nor serrated on its rim. **Introduced into the region** from eastern parts of South Africa. Moves slowly about a home range of between 1 and 2 km², feeding on plant foliage and berries. Females lay clutches of ping-pong ball-sized eggs in shallow burrows. Young are vulnerable to many predators, and adults to grass fires.
Length: up to 72 cm

SF **M**

Marsh Terrapin

Semi-aquatic terrapin with a flattened shell. The **neck is folded sideways** under the shell. Several individuals may occupy a dam or pond, where they bask on rocks. Often moves over land, particularly after rain. Spends the dry season buried in soil. Feeds on a wide variety of other animals including frogs, tadpoles and birds, and often scavenges. Oval eggs are laid in a burrow.
Length: 20 to 30 cm

W D HAACKE

M F

Ocellated Gecko

Small chubby gecko with **dark chocolate-brown back dotted with creamy-white spots**. The toes are wide and flattened with tiny pads which allow it to cling to smooth surfaces. **Nocturnal**, shy and secretive. Usually occurs among rocks or fallen logs in damp situations. Feeds on a variety of insects and spiders which are captured after a short chase. A pair of tiny white eggs are laid under cover.
Length: 7 cm

C & T STUART

GP F M

Marbled Leaftoed Gecko

Small flattened gecko with **mottled, pale brown back** sometimes with a bold, pale stripe down the middle. A dark band may run through the eye of some individuals. The toes are splayed with a pair of split pads which allow it to cling to smooth surfaces. **Nocturnal** but not shy; numbers may gather on walls of houses around outdoor lights. Feeds on moths and other insects. Hides in cracks by day.
Length: 9 cm

C & T STUART

M GP F

Cape Dwarf Chameleon

Medium-sized, shrub-dwelling chameleon, and the only member of the family to occur in the vicinity of Cape Town. The **colour varies** from leaf-green to pale grey, usually with an orange lateral stripe. The **conical eyes** move independently of one another, and the long tail is used as a fifth limb. Insect prey is captured with the long sticky tongue. Live young are produced.
Length: 15 cm

Cape Girdled Lizard

Small, **black or dark brown** lizard with a flattened body and **flat triangular head**. The back is covered in rows of keeled scales and the **tail is spiny**. Most active in mornings and evenings. Lives among rocks and is common on the slopes of Table Mountain and at Cape Point where individuals look out from atop stones and boulders. Feeds on beetles and other insects.
Length: 13 to 19 cm

M

Southern Rock Agama

Medium-sized lizard with a squat body, triangular head and thin tail. The breeding male is dull black with a pale stripe down the middle of its back and tail; the **head is blue-green** and the throat turquoise. Females and non-breeding males are dull grey-brown with a blue throat. Occurs in colonies among rocks often alongside the Cape Girdled Lizard. Active by day.
Length: 20 to 25 cm

RS   **M**

Cape (Threelined) Skink

Chubby, pale-bodied lizard with long tapering tail. **Three off-white stripes** run the length of the grey-buff body; the underbelly is off-white. **Active by day**, it occurs in open habitats where it hunts large insects such as grasshoppers, beetles and termites. It tunnels in loose sand but may also take refuge under rocks and logs. Interestingly, the young may be born live or out of eggs.
Length: 25 cm

C & T STUART

GP   **M**   **SF**

Redsided (Orangelegged) Skink

Slender, variably coloured lizard with long tapering tail. The back and head are dark brown or fawn with a **broad black and narrow red stripe** on each flank. In some breeding males the limbs turn orange-red. Active by day. Occurs singly or in small groups, foraging on the ground in search of termites and other insects. Wary and quick to scurry for cover when approached.
Length: 15 to 18 cm

W D HAACKE

SF   **M**

73

PETER LAWSON

M **SF** **GP**

Brown House Snake

Medium-sized snake which occurs in most habitats, and also in buildings where it preys on rodents. The squared-off snout and **two pale lines on either side of the pale eye** are diagnostic. Body colour is variable, ranging from light brown to rust, becoming darker with age. Prey is killed by constriction, then swallowed head first. Nocturnal. Up to 15 eggs are laid in summer.
Length: 1 m (max. 1.5 m)

WD HAACKE

WR **M** **SF**

Common Egg-eater

Small, boldly marked snake characterised by **two dark V-patterns on the top of the head** (that nearest the neck being boldest). Often associated with old termite mounds in which it shelters by day. In a remarkable dietary adaptation, the jaws can expand to engulf birds' eggs, larger than its own head, which may then be swallowed. It lacks sizeable teeth and cannot bite. Up to 25 eggs are laid.
Length: 50 to 70 cm (max. 1 m)

WD HAACKE

WR **GP** **M**

Herald Snake

Small slender snake with glossy, blue-black head and **yellow sides of upper lip**. The body is uniformly olive-brown above, sometimes with small white spots; the underbelly is off-white. This snake has adapted well to suburbia and is sometimes uncovered among garden litter or rubble. **Nocturnal**. It feeds mostly upon frogs so is most at home in wetlands. Up to 12 eggs are laid in summer.
Length: 60 to 75 cm (max. 80 cm)

WD HAACKE

F **GP** **M**

Boomslang (Tree Snake) ☠

Long thin snake **characterised by big eyes**. Males are bright or dull green with variable black and pale blue markings. Females are pale olive-brown. Juveniles are greyish with a white chin, yellow throat and green eyes. Active by day. It spends almost all of its time in trees, feeding mostly on birds and dwarf chameleons. Shy, but extremely dangerous if handled – the venom may prove fatal to man.
Length: 1 to 2 m

74

Mole Snake

Large, thick-bodied snake with **short pointed snout**. Adults in the Cape are pitch-black; juveniles are attractively patterned in tan and black. **Active by day**, it preys on burrowing mammals in their holes. Victims are constricted before being swallowed. Non-poisonous, but able to inflict severe bites in self-defence. Gives birth to 30 to 50 live young in autumn.

Length: 1.5 m (max. 2 m)

W D HAACKE

M **SF**

Rinkhals 🕱

Large snake with orange-brown tiger pattern and **keeled scales**. The underside is black with white bars on the throat. This dangerous snake more often **sprays venom** than bites. If threatened it will rise and spread its cobra-like hood; it **may sham death** if the threat persists. Feeds mostly on toads, but will also take rodents and even other snakes. Up to 30 live young are born in summer.

Length: up to 1.5 m

W D HAACKE

SF **WR** **M**

Cape Cobra 🕱

Large slender snake with different colour forms in different parts of southern Africa. On the Cape Peninsula most are **reddish-brown with paler or darker speckles**; juveniles are pale fawn with a dark throat band. Active by day but shy and nervous. When threatened it **spreads its hood** as a warning but may bite if cornered or molested (it does not spray) to inject its potentially fatal venom.

Length: up to 1.5 m

W D HAACKE

SF

Puff Adder 🕱

Stocky snake with **chevron patterns in ochre, tan and black**. The scales are keeled, giving a rough appearance and texture. Although most active at dusk and after dark, it may be encountered by day. Rodents, frogs and ground birds are the main prey. Litters consist of 20 to 40 young. It is sluggish but will bite readily, usually below the knee. The venom is potentially fatal to man.

Length: 1 m ss: Berg Adder; Manyhorned Adder

W D HAACKE

SF **M**

75

Frogs

Some twenty species of frog occur in the Cape Town area, of which more than half are restricted to this winter-rainfall tip of the continent. Nine of the more commonly encountered species are featured in this section, along with the extremely rare and endangered Table Mountain Ghost Frog which has become the symbolic victim of the environmental threats facing the Peninsula. Among the frogs not included is the tiny Micro Frog which was once common in shallow pans of the Cape Flats but may now be locally extinct.

Frogs are fascinating creatures to study providing that one is not afraid of getting a little muddy or wet and is prepared to capture the slippery customers by hand (to be released after study or photography). Like birds, frogs have distinctive calls and this is of help in their location and identification. Most are only active after dark, however, and are best found by going out at night with a strong torch after, or during, rain. Frogs are, of course, best known for having two stages in life: the tadpole (larval), which is usually totally aquatic, and the four-limbed adult, which may be active in or out of water.

The aquatic habitats favoured by frogs are at risk from drainage for development and pollution. A drop in frog numbers indicates that the environment as a whole is in poor shape and this must be of concern to all Capetonians. The names used here follow those in *South African Frogs – A Complete Guide* by Passmore and Carruthers (Southern and Wits Univ. Press, 1995); a compact disc entitled *Voices of South African Frogs* augments this work. The little booklet – *Frogs of the Western Cape* by Peter Slingsby (Ekko) – is a useful regional publication.

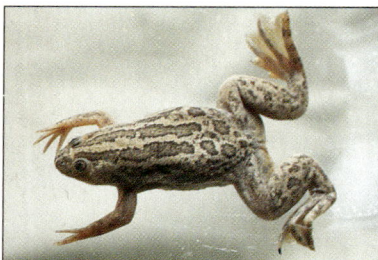

VINCENT CARRUTHERS

WR

Cape Platanna

Unusual frog with compressed body and **eyes on the top of its head**. Often seen suspended just below the water surface. The fore limbs are short and slender, but the legs are powerful with webbing between the **clawed toes**. Confined to the south-western Cape where it inhabits **shallow pans**. The **Common Platanna** has now invaded these water bodies and out-competes this smaller species.
Length: up to 8 cm ss: Common Platanna (12 cm)

VINCENT CARRUTHERS

SF

Cape Rain Frog (Blaasop)

Rotund frog with a tiny head. When handled or molested, it typically **inflates its body into a ball-shape**. The back is buffy-brown and granular with cream flanks; the underside is pale cream and mottled. Emerges from underground burrow only after rain. The call is an abrupt squawk repeated every few seconds. The smaller **Sand Rain Frog** has black streaks behind its eyes.
Length: 5 to 6 cm ss: Sand Rain Frog (3 cm)

Raucous Toad

Sandy-brown or grey toad with **dark uneven blotches on a putty-coloured back**. The skin on the back is lumpy and the underside is off-white and granular. Occurs most often alongside running water but also visits ponds and dams. Strictly nocturnal. The call is a sharp 'kwaak', repeated at intervals – **usually uttered from the water's edge**, or in nearby vegetation
Length: 5 to 7 cm ss: Leopard Toad (10 cm)

GP   WR

Sand Toad

Small, boldly marked toad with dark blotches on a fawn back. Distinguished from other toads by the **yellow upper surface of the back feet**. The skin on the back is lumpy and the underside is off-white and granular. A thin pale line down the middle of the back is usually present. Occurs in shallow waterlogged depressions. The call is a nasal 'gnyee', repeated every few seconds.
Length: 5 to 6 cm ss: Cape Mountain Toad

SF

Cape Sand Frog

Small chubby frog attractively patterned in white and grey-brown, with darker raised bumps on the back. A thin, pale stripe may be conspicuous on its back. Close examination in the hand reveals a **small ridge on each hind foot** which is used for digging in sand. Favours the edges of pans, dams and lagoons in sandy areas. Males call from cover with a monotonous ringing note.
Length: 4 cm

GP   SF   WR

Cape Chirping Frog

Tiny frog associated with damp mossy areas near streams or waterfalls. The back is variable in colour, with or without a thin middle stripe and with black streaks behind each eye. The underside may be white, black or marbled. The toes are not webbed. Tadpoles do not swim in open water, but develop within moist vegetation. The call is a cricket-like chirp, repeated at intervals.
Length: 2 cm ss: Common Caco; Cape Caco

WR

WR M

Cape River Frog

Streamlined frog with **pointed snout**. The **hind legs are long** and **the toes well-webbed**. The back is variable in colour, often with a thin middle stripe. Occurs in still or flowing water usually resting on the bank or rocks; it leaps into the water with a splash when approached. Common in streams on the top of Table Mountain. The call is a series of taps followed by a sharp grunt.
Length: up to 8 cm

WR

Clicking Stream Frog

Streamlined frog with **sharply pointed snout**. The **hind legs are extremely long and slender** and **the toes are only slightly webbed**. The back is variable in colour, usually blotched with a thin middle stripe; the underside is plain white. Occurs in fringing vegetation alongside still or flowing water. The monotonous tapping call is a familiar sound on damp winter nights in Cape Town.
Length: 4 to 5 cm ss: Banded Stream Frog

M

Table Mountain Ghost Frog

Small frog with long limbs and **toes that end in distinctive spatulate pads**. The back is green with purple markings. **Occurs only in perennial streams edged with forest on the eastern slopes of Table Mountain** where it is rare and seldom seen due to its cryptic colouration and habit of hiding in crevices. Call is a repetitive ringing note. Endangered due to reservoir construction and alien plants.
Length: 4 cm

WR

Arumlily Frog

Tiny frog with slender legs and arms. The **toes and fingers end in rounded discs** which enable it to cling to slippery surfaces. The back is usually cream coloured, but some individuals are pale brown. A dark band usually runs down each flank. The **inner thighs and toe and finger webbing is bright orange**. Occurs in fringing vegetation around pans, often sitting in arumlily blooms. The call is a repetitive harsh bleat.
Length: 3 to 4 cm

Freshwater Fishes

The south-western Cape is not endowed with a great diversity of freshwater fishes, although 14 species are endemic to streams and rivers in the fynbos biome. As man has developed the area many rivers and streams have become polluted or dammed by reservoirs, while a variety of alien fish species have been introduced for recreational angling purposes. Since many of these fishes are predatory, they have impacted severely on populations of smaller indigenous fish. At least one species of redfin minnow has become extinct in recent years, while the Berg River Redfin has been eliminated from the Eerste River near Stellenbosch, and is regarded as one of South Africa's most endangered fishes.

On the Cape Peninsula itself, naturalists and anglers are more likely to encounter or catch alien fishes than indigenous ones. For this reason, four of the six species featured in this section are native to other regions. Among the indigenous species not featured are the Longfin Eel and the Whitefish.

A fascinating freshwater exhibit at the Two Oceans Aquarium contains various indigenous fishes from the south-western Cape, and clearly shows how certain species occupy specific zones of river systems. This exhibit affords the best opportunity of seeing indigenous species, unless you net and release fish in a stream or wetland.

Names used in this section follow those in *A Complete Guide to the Freshwater Fishes of Southern Africa* by Paul Skelton (Southern, 1993). This is the most comprehensive and easy-to-use guide to the 245 indigenous and introduced freshwater fishes, and contains detailed information on ecology.

Cape Galaxias

Tiny, cigar-shaped fish with **small dorsal fin set far back** above the anal fin. The body lacks scales and is remarkably **translucent** with heart, gills and other organs being visible. Favours moving water close to banks where it can shelter and retreat from predators. Very hardy and able to withstand a range of water conditions and temperatures. Feeds on aquatic invertebrates. **Threatened**.
Length: 40 to 75 mm

PAUL SKELTON

WR

Carp *

Very large, pale olive to bronze fish. **Native to Asia**, this species was first introduced into South Africa in 1859. It is now naturalised and widespread in still or slow-moving water. Feeds on a wide variety of plants and aquatic creatures. A favoured angling species, but it causes damage to aquatic food-chains. The popular Koi is an ornamental variation of the Carp.
Length: up to 80 cm SA record mass: 21 kg

R A JUBB

WR

Cape Kurper

Smallish, spear-shaped fish with a blunt snout. Bronze-brown with **black spots and bands on the flanks and black stripes radiating from the eyes**. Breeding males become dark brown or black. The dorsal fin is long and serrated, the tail fin is undivided. Favours quiet, slow-moving waters where it preys on invertebrates. Males defend their territory and guard eggs. **Threatened**.
Length: 20 cm

PAUL SKELTON

Mozambique Tilapia *

Medium-sized, omnivorous fish with a **long dorsal fin fringed with spines**. Adults are silvery-olive with dorsal and tail fins tipped in red; breeding male is dark grey-black with a white throat. Male builds a bowl-shaped 'nest' on sandy bottoms, and the female broods eggs and young in her mouth. **Native to the eastern parts of South Africa**, but introduced into the Peninsula.
Length: 40 cm SA record mass: 3.2 kg

PAUL SKELTON

Largemouth Bass *

Large, pale olive fish with dark bands. **Native to North America**, this is one of the world's most popular sport fishes, and was introduced into this country in 1928. The **deeply cleft dorsal fin** is distinctive. Found in dams or slow-moving rivers, and favours clear water with floating vegetation. A predator of other fish, but also takes crabs and frogs – they are a hazard to indigenous fauna.
Length: up to 60 cm SA record mass: 4.5 kg

PAUL SKELTON

Bluegill Sunfish *

Smallish, round-bodied fish with steep forehead. Colour varies but is usually green-blue with indistinct vertical bars. In breeding males, the **underparts are bright orange** and the mouth pale blue. **Native to North America**, it was introduced into South Africa as fodder for the Largemouth Bass. Favours still water with emergent vegetation where it feeds on smaller fish and invertebrates.
Length: up to 20 cm

Marine Fishes

A great diversity and abundance of marine fishes occur in the waters surrounding the Cape Peninsula, with different species favouring different conditions created by water depth, turbulence and temperature. The greatest concentration of fishes occur over the continental shelf along the west coast, and this is where the country's commercial fishing industry is based. Fishes such as the Sardine and Shad follow seasonal movements and are common at certain times of the year and absent at others.

Fishes are traditionally of more interest to anglers than they are to naturalists but this situation appears to be changing as more people take up scuba diving and underwater photography as a hobby – a fascinating array of herbivores, predators and scavengers occupy niches in the underwater ecosystems. For those not inclined to seek out fishes in their natural habitat, however, much can be learned from a visit to the excellent Two Oceans Aquarium at the Cape Town Waterfront. Here, one can observe most of the fishes featured in this section, and very much more besides, without getting wet!

Only a handful of the more common or distinctive species are featured on the following pages so the enthusiast will need a copy of *A Guide to Common Sea Fishes of Southern Africa* by Van der Elst (Struik, 1985) or the comprehensive tome – *Smiths' Sea Fishes* revised by Smith and Heemstra (Southern, 1988). The excellent *Two Oceans: A Guide to the Marine Life of South Africa* by Branch, Griffiths and others (David Philip, 1994) includes most of the familiar marine fishes found in southern Africa.

Raggedtooth Shark

Large, torpedo-shaped fish with conical snout. The **dorsal and anal fins are large**; the tail fin is sickle-shaped. The rough body skin is brownish above, paler below. The teeth are fang-like. Forages close to shore, feeding on fishes and crustaceans. Said to be dangerous only if provoked. The massive **Great White Shark** has a tiny anal fin, large pectoral fins, and is blueish-grey in colour.
Length: 3 m ss: Great White Shark (up to 6 m)

Blue Stingray ☠

Flat, disc-shaped fish related to sharks. The scaleless skin of the upperside is sandy-yellow with blue mottling; the underside is pale. The **whip-like tail** is armed with a poison-bearing spine. Occurs in shallow sandy bays where it is extremely well camouflaged, and preys mostly on bottom-dwelling crustaceans. Other rays off the south-western Cape coast are the **Eagleray** and **Bullray**.
Width: up to 75 cm

PHIL HEEMSTRA

Sardine (Pilchard)

Cigar-shaped fish with large eyes. The body is silvery-blue with a row of 10 to 15 **small black spots on the flanks**. Small fins are transparent and spineless. **Forms huge shoals** which feed mostly on plankton. Important prey item for seabirds, seals and dolphins, and is the 'backbone' of the pelagic fishing industry. Migrates up the east coast on its 'sardine run' each winter.

Length: up to 30 cm ss: Round Herring; Cape Anchovy

Kingklip

Eel-like fish with narrow dorsal and anal fins joined at the tail. The body is pinkish with brown blotches; paler below. Soft scales do not overlap; slimy to handle. Forages on the ocean floor in **deeper waters**. Small, bottom-dwelling fish and crustaceans make up the bulk of its diet. A valued table fish; large numbers are trawled off the west coast and Namibia.

Length: up to 1.5 m

Yellowbelly Rock Cod

Robust fish with variable colouration and a large mouth. The yellow-margined **dorsal fin has 11 strong spines**; the tail fin is slightly rounded. The body is dark brown and mottled above; **yellow below**. Favours rocky shores and reefs. Solitary predator of bottom-dwelling fish, octopus and crustaceans. Popular angling fish and fine eating but at risk of over-exploitation.

Length: up to 1.5 m Minimum catch size: 30 cm

Roman

Deep-bodied fish with a large mouth. The body is **orange-red with a distinctive white saddle on the back**, a white bar on the gill covers, and a blue stripe between the eyes. The dorsal fin is jagged with 11 or 12 spines; the tail is forked. Bottom-dwelling predator of invertebrates. Occurs mostly east of Cape Point. Popular angling fish and fine eating.

Length: 30 to 50 cm Minimum catch size: 25 cm

PHIL HEEMSTRA

PHIL HEEMSTRA

82

Red Stumpnose

Medium-sized fish with a distinctive **sloping forehead**; older males often develop a pronounced forehead bump. The deep body is silvery-white in colour with broad, orange-red vertical bars. The dorsal fin has 11 or 12 spines at the front, the tail fin is deeply forked. Usually occurs singly in deeper reefs where it preys mostly upon molluscs and crustaceans.

Length: up to 60 cm Minimum catch size: 25 cm

Cape Salmon (Geelbek)

Torpedo-shaped fish with a **distinctive yellow mouth and gill cover**. The body is silvery-grey above, somewhat paler below. Favours deeper water where it occurs in shoals that prey mostly on smaller fish; many follow the 'sardine run' up the east coast to KwaZulu-Natal during the winter months. Caught mostly by ski-boat fishermen; a much relished table fish.

Length: up to 1.2 m Minimum catch size: 40 cm

Kob (Kabeljou)

Elongated fish with a sloped head. The body is silver with a pinkish sheen on the head and upperparts. The **dorsal fin is divided into two** with the front section having 10 spines; the tail fin is squared-off. Gregarious, shoaling predator of small fish and crustaceans. Often found in murky water close to shore and in estuaries. Popular angling fish and exploited by trawlers; fine eating.

Length: up to 2 m Minimum catch size: 40 cm

Strepie (Karanteen)

Oval fish with a pointed snout. Body is silvery-green with **8 to 10 thin yellow stripes running from head to tail**. The dorsal fin has 11 spines, the tail is deeply cleft. Occurs in shoals, favouring shallow rocky areas. Juveniles feed mostly on tiny crustaceans, adults feed almost entirely on seaweed. One of the most abundant herbivorous fishes. Popular with anglers and good eating.

Length: 30 to 40 cm ss: Steentjie; Hottentot

Galjoen (Damba)

Deep-bodied fish with colour varying from **silvery-bronze to black**. Faint bars may be visible on the flanks. The front part of the dorsal fin is divided from the hind section which matches the anal fin and tapers toward the tail. Occurs in turbulent water; omnivorous. **National fish of South Africa**. Popular angling fish but now a **protected species** which may not be caught in summer.

Length: up to 80 cm Minimum catch size: 35 cm

Garrick (Leervis)

Elongated fish with a pointed snout and tiny scales giving a **smooth leathery texture**. The body is silvery-green with a **distinctive, dark, wavy line on the flanks**. The dorsal fin is divided into two with the rear section similar to match the anal fin; the tail is deeply cleft. Pack-hunting predator of smaller fish, favouring the surf zone. Favoured angling fish; fair eating.

Length: up to 1.5 m Minimum catch size: 70 cm

Shad (Elf)

Elongated fish with a pointed snout. The body is silvery-green but turns blue when dead. The dorsal fin is divided into two, with front section having 7 or 8 small spines and the **hind section similar to the anal fin**; the tail is deeply cleft. Shoaling predator of small fish; follows the 'sardine run' to KwaZulu-Natal in winter. Population appears to be recovering from over-exploitation.

Length: up to 1 m Minimum catch size: 30 cm

PHIL HEEMSTRA

Snoek

Spear-shaped fish with a pointed snout. The body is silver with a thin, dark, wavy line on the flanks. The long, dark grey dorsal fin is broadest at the back of the head, tapering to the deeply cleft tail fin; spines on the dorsal fin are silver. Shoaling predator of small fish and krill; most frequent beyond the continental shelf. Caught by anglers and commercial fishers; fine eating, best smoked.

Length: up to 1.5 m Minimum catch size: 60 cm

Southern Mullet (Harder)

Elongated fish with a pointed snout. The body is silvery-white, darker on the back, with a distinctive **yellow spot on each gill cover**. Two pointed **dorsal fins are set well apart**; the black tail fin is slightly forked. Occurs in shoals, mostly in shallow water; **frequent in estuaries** which are used as nurseries. Feeds on diatoms. Caught commercially in nets, it is a delicacy when smoked.
Length: 40 cm

O

Maned Blenny

Small chubby fish with **square head** tapering to a narrow tail. Body is variable in colour with dark crossbars and blotches; it is **scaleless** and slimy to the touch. A **'mane' of short tentacles** appears above the eyes. The long dorsal and anal fins are frilled and meet at the tail. It feeds on algae in tidal pools and shallow water on rocky shores. Eggs are guarded by the male.
Length: 10 cm

PHIL HEEMSTRA

RS

Evileyed Puffer (Blaasop) ☠

Chubby, scaleless fish with **dark green back** freckled in white, and white under-side separated by a **pale yellow lateral band**. The **eyes are green**. Inflates itself if molested. Favours shallow, sandy areas **east of Cape Point**. Ambushes crabs and invertebrates, and scavenges morsels. Frequently robs the bait of surf-fishers. Flesh is highly toxic and should not be eaten or fed to animals.
Length: 13 cm

RS

Bareheaded Goby

Small elongated fish with a **rounded head**. It has **no tentacles** above the eyes. Body is mottled in shades of fawn, grey and brown. The dorsal fin is divided into two, and the pelvic fin is modified to form a sucking disc. A resident of tidal pools where it feeds on algae and small invertebrates. Eggs are attached to the surface of pebbles or shells.
Length: 14 cm ss: Rocksucker (30 cm)

PHIL HEEMSTRA

RS

85

Marine Invertebrates

Exploring the shore is one of the most fascinating pursuits for the naturalist and a great diversity of interesting creatures may be found around the Cape Peninsula. Rock pools and exposed reefs support the greatest abundance of marine invertebrates, with most being confined to specific zones which relate to the degree of exposure and wave action. Sandy beaches are less interesting, although concentrations of some organisms occur from time to time, and stranded jellyfish and other creatures are often washed ashore.

Marine invertebrates are separated into a number of main divisions (phyla) of which the **sponges**, **cnidarians** (anemones, corals and jellyfish), **arthropods** (barnacles, isopods, lobsters, crabs), **molluscs** (bivalves, chitons, limpets, whelks, nudibranchs, octopus, squid) and **echinoderms** (starfish, brittlestars, sea urchins, sea cucumbers) are the best known. All of these creatures differ from 'higher' animal groups in the lack of an internal skeleton. The identification of invertebrates often requires close study, but the commonly encountered species featured in this section should pose few problems. For more detailed study, the excellent *Two Oceans: A Guide to the Marine Life of Southern Africa* by Branch, Griffiths, Branch and Beckley (David Philip, 1994) and *The Living Shores of Southern Africa* by Branch, Branch and Bannister (Struik, 1981) are indispensable books.

Marine invertebrates are best seen at low tide, when much of the shoreline is exposed and many creatures are temporarily confined to small rockpools. The tide rises and falls twice each day, allowing the observer time to access the lower reaches at least once during daylight hours. The variation from low to high tide is most pronounced at the time of the full and new moon, when spring-tides occur; this is the best time of all for exploration.

The intertidal reaches of rocky shores are divided into four band-like zones determined by their distance from the sea: the **Littorina Zone** which is seldom submerged and supports mostly small snails; the **Upper Balanoid Zone** which is dominated by limpets or barnacles; the **Lower Balanoid Zone** which is dominated by mussels and seaweeds; and the **Cochlear Zone** where Pear Limpets are the dominant lifeforms.

Sponges

Colourful, primitive animals which live on rocks in intertidal pools or below low tide zone. They filter fine food particles from water pumped through their porous outer surface.

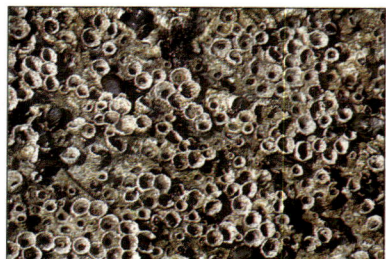

Cape Reef Worm

Small gregarious creature which lives in a specially constructed tube of sand grains and shell particles. **Forms large colonies or 'reefs'** on rocky shores. Filters micro-organisms from waves.

False Plum Anemone

Dark red anemone which lives in crevices and rock pools on rocky shores where it is never exposed. Its stinging tentacles are used to stun prey. The smaller **Plum Anemone** is often exposed at low tide.
Diameter: up to 10 cm ss: Plum Anemone (2 cm)

Sandy Anemone

Variably coloured anemone which occurs in sandy bottomed rock pools. Tentacles may be pale green, yellow, red or mauve. Sand and shell particles adhere to its sticky body. Prey is varied.
Diameter: 8 cm

Rootmouthed Jellyfish

Mushroom-shaped jellyfish with gelatinous, translucent blue body. Most often seen washed ashore dead. Unusual among jellyfish, it has no stinging tentacles; tiny prey is sieved through pores.
Diameter: 30 cm (max. 1.5 m)

Bluebottle ☠

Not a single animal, but a colony of individuals of which one is a translucent blue gas-filled float. Tubular individuals occur as tentacles with poisonous stinging cells for prey capture. Often washed ashore.
Length: float 5 cm; tentacles 30 cm to 10 m

Red Bait

Ascidian, or sea squirt, with wrinkled, dark brown skin. May form colonies on rocks on the mid-shore. Feeds by filtering water sucked in one siphon and expelled from the other. Red flesh is used as bait.
Length: 15 cm (but can be much larger)

Mediterranean Mussel *

Mollusc with a pair of dark shells joined with a hinge. Occurs in colonies; **mostly in the mid-shore**. Invader **native to Europe**; outnumbers indigenous **Black** and **Brown Mussels** on the Peninsula.
Length: up to 14 cm

87

CHARLES GRIFFITHS

White Mussel (Wedge Shell)

Mollusc protected within a pair of creamy-white, wedge-shaped shells; wavy ridges run across the upper end. Favours sandy beaches with strong wave action. Good eating and fish-bait.

Length: 8 cm (minimum catch: 35 mm)

Goose Barnacle

Crustacean encased in five overlapping, glossy white shells. Occurs in colonies; attaches itself by a tough stalk to ships, driftwood or other floating objects. Feathery limbs capture tiny prey.

Length: 3 cm

Volcano Barnacle

Crustacean protected within a grey, volcano-shaped shell which consists of ridged plates. Attaches itself to rocks in the intertidal zone. Occurs in colonies. Feathery limbs capture tiny prey.

Length: 2 cm

Eight-shell Barnacle

Crustacean protected within an off-white shell of eight plates. Attaches itself to rocks in the intertidal zone. Occurs in densely packed colonies. Feathery limbs capture tiny prey.

Length: 2 cm

Venus Ear (Siffie)

Mollusc protected within an off-white, ear-shaped shell with a row of small holes near its rim. The inside of the shell is a beautiful 'mother-of-pearl' colour. Found at low tide on wave-exposed reefs.

Length: 8 cm (minimum catch: 35 mm)

Perlemoen (Abalone)

Mollusc within a flattened, ear-shaped shell with a row of small holes near the rim; interior is mother-of-pearl. Young live in rock pools, adults common in kelp beds. Relished seafood.

Diameter: up to 19 cm (minimum catch: 12 cm at 13 years of age. Protected – permit required)

CHARLES GRIFFITHS

Granular Limpet

Mollusc with an oval, **dome-shaped shell with raised ribs**. The inside of the shell is blue-white with a dark centre. Occurs in colonies on rocks. Similar **Bearded Limpet** has protruding ribs.

Diameter: 8 cm ss: Bearded Limpet (8 cm)

Pear Limpet

Mollusc with a distinctive, **pear-shaped shell**, often covered in crusty algae. Occurs in colonies on exposed rocks where it dominates the Cochlear Zone. Grazes on paint-like algae.

Diameter: 7 cm

Cape False Limpet

Mollusc with an oval shell swollen on one side. Dark ribs radiate from the apex but **do not protrude** beyond the margin. Occurs in pools and on rocks in the mid-shore; tolerant of sand cover.

Diameter: 2 cm

Variegated Topshell

Small, snail-like mollusc with a variably patterned, rounded shell. Occurs in colonies on rocks in the upper shore. Individuals are constantly on the move, feeding on algae.

Diameter: 1 cm ss: African Periwinkle (1 cm)

Alikreukel (Giant Periwinkle)

Mollusc with a large, **turban-shaped shell**. The entrance is closed by a knob-bly white disc – often found washed up on the shore. Feeds on algae. Good eating but catch size is restricted.

Diameter: 10 cm (minimum catch: 64 mm)

Ridged Burnupena

Dark, snail-like mollusc with about six ridges at the tip of its shell which is often covered in green algae. Crawls around on rocks near the low tide, where it scavenges on dead creatures.

Length: 4 cm

BETH PETERSON/AFRICAN IMAGES

Finger Ploughshell

One of several species of ploughshell in the area. The flesh-coloured shell is smooth and the 'foot' broad and flat. Occurs on sandy, wave-exposed beaches, where it scavenges on carrion located by scent.
Length: 6 cm

BETH PETERSON/AFRICAN IMAGES

Violet Snail

Mollusc within a delicate spiral shell which varies in colour from lilac to mauve. Hangs upside down on sea surface, suspended by air bubbles. Preys on bluebottles. Shells often washed ashore.
Diameter: 3 cm

Spiny Chiton

Flattened, slug-like mollusc with eight overlapping plates on its back. Spiny outgrowths protrude from the leathery girdle. Occurs on rocks in the intertidal zone. Ten related species occur in the area.
Length: 3 to 7 cm

CHARLES GRIFFITHS

Common Cuttlefish

Ten-limbed mollusc resembling a squid. Its two long feeding limbs are armed with stinging cells to immobilise fish prey. The chalky internal shell of dead individuals is often washed ashore.
Length: 15 cm

CHARLES GRIFFITHS

Common Octopus

Distinctive, eight-limbed mollusc with two rows of suckers on each tentacle or limb. Territorial. Hides in rock pools and on reefs, ambushing crabs and lobsters. Grows to full size within a year.
Length: 60 cm

CAPE NATURE CONSERVATION

Chokka Squid

Cigar-shaped mollusc with eight short arms and two long tentacles at the mouth. Fins extend from the sides of the mantle. Preys on small fish. Rarely washed ashore; caught by 'jigging' with lures.
Length: 20 to 30 cm

Dwarf Cushionstar

Small, flattened echinoderm with short triangular arms. Colour and pattern vary greatly. Extremely well camouflaged in rock pools where it feeds on algae. Eggs are laid on the undersides of rocks.
Diameter: 2 cm ss: Subtidal Cushionstar (4 cm)

Elegant Feather Star

Graceful echinoderm with ten feathery arms arising from a small body. Usually yellow in colour. Attaches itself to a rock, feeding on micro-organisms which are filtered from the water by tentacles.
Length of arms: up to 15 cm

Spiny Starfish

Large, blue-grey or orange starfish with five arms. The upperside is covered in knobbly spines. Occurs in pools on rocky shores. Preys upon mussels and other shellfish.
Diameter: 20 cm

CHARLES GRIFFITHS

Red Starfish

Globular, orange-red starfish with five shortish arms. The body texture is scaly. Occurs on rocks, moving slowly on its tube-like feet which are also used to feed on detritus.
Diameter: 9 cm

CHARLES GRIFFITHS

Serpentskinned Brittlestar

Flattened, spider-like echinoderm with five elongated, spine-tipped arms which are brittle and break off easily if handled. Occurs singly or in groups under rocks in rock pools. Feeds on detritus.
Diameter: 5 cm

CHARLES GRIFFITHS

Redchested Sea Cucumber

Sausage-shaped echinoderm without the typical star-shape of its relatives. Captures tiny organisms with its tentacles. Intertidal specimens are dark above; subtidal specimens are all red.
Length: 2 to 4 cm

Cape Urchin

Round echinoderm covered in pointed spines which may be mauve, red, green or pink in colour. Lives in rockpools where it feeds on algae. Pale green, internal shells are often washed ashore.

Diameter: 2 to 6 cm

Sea Slater

Louse-like crustacean which occurs in large congregations on rocky shores and among drift kelp. Feeds on detritus. Individuals in groups are usually of different sizes, reflecting age classes.

Length: up to 2 cm

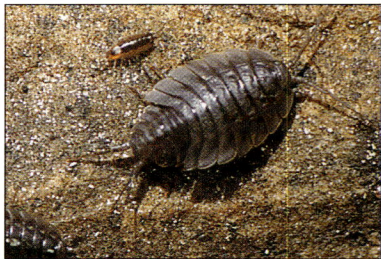

West Coast Rock Lobster

Ten-legged crustacean with long antennae and fanned tail. Occurs in well aerated water of reefs and rocky shores. Preys on mussels and urchins. Relished seafood; popularly known as crayfish.

Length: 30 cm (min. catch: 75 mm carapace length)

Cape Rock Crab

Reddish-brown crab with two distinctive notches between the eyes, pale ridges on the legs, and white spots on the pincers. Occurs in pools and shallow reefs, feeding on seaweed and small invertebrates.

Carapace width: 5 cm

Shore Crab

Smooth-bodied crab with orange-brown carapace. The orange legs are finely spotted in brown. Usually keeps to the upper shore where it feeds mostly on detritus after dark.

Carapace width: 3 cm

European Shore Crab *

Khaki-green crab **native to Europe,** introduced accidentally and now spreading up the Atlantic coast. Occurs in areas protected from waves. Preys on molluscs, posing a threat to the shellfish industry.

Carapace width: 5 cm

Land and Freshwater Invertebrates

Not surprisingly, a great variety of spiders, insects and other invertebrates occur on the Cape Peninsula. The accurate identification of these creatures is often a complex matter, however, and is beyond the scope of this book. On the following pages, only a handful of the most conspicuous creatures are featured with the emphasis on the identification of groups rather than species.

Invertebrates abound in almost all habitats and one way to learn about them is to capture specimens by sweeping through vegetation with a fine-gauze net, or by attracting them to an outdoor light after dark. Useful books to refer to for more detailed information are *African Insect Life* revised by Skaife, revised by Ledger (Struik, 1979), *Pocket Guide: Insects* by Holm (Struik, 1986) and *Southern African Spiders: An Identification Guide* by Filmer (Struik, 1991).

Apart from being interesting in their own right, many insects play a vital role in the reproductive cycle of plants. Recent research has demonstrated, for example, that certain ants are important agents in the dispersal of seeds of fynbos plants.

River crabs

Freshwater crabs which move readily over land at night, or after rain. Favour rocky streams where carrion, small fish and tadpoles are eaten. Predators include the Giant Kingfisher.
Carapace width: up to 10 cm

Garden snails

Small molluscs with a thin brittle shell which keeps the body moist. Feed on leaves and buds, so are considered pests in gardens. Most active in wet weather and after dark.
Length: up to 5 cm

Centipedes

Flattened arthropods with outspread legs. Active after dark when they move in a snake-like fashion. Colour varies from yellow to tan or blue. Tail pincers are used in defence. Prey on insects.
Length: up to 10 cm

Millipedes

Cylindrical arthropods with hair-like legs. Movement is fairly slow, but avoided by most predators as they eject a pungent, toxic fluid. Curl into a spiral when threatened. Feed on plant material.
Length: up to 15 cm

Orbweb spiders

Large, usually yellow and black spiders which construct classic hanging webs to ensnare prey. The webs of larger species may be strong enough to hold small birds. Males are tiny compared to females.

Rain (Wandering) spiders

Velvety spiders with long hairy legs. Hunt cockroaches and other insects after dark. Often come into houses during or after rain. Eggs are protected within a woven pouch of leaves.

Flower crab spiders

Small, triangular-bodied spiders which ambush insect prey – sometimes much larger than themselves – in flowers which match their own body colour; usually pink, white or yellow.

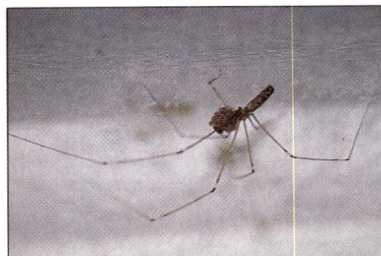

Daddy-longlegs spiders

Small-bodied spiders with extremely long legs. Common in houses where they build their webs in corners. Most active after dark when they feed upon a variety of smaller creatures.

Dragonflies

Helicopter-like insects associated with fresh water. Many are brightly coloured in red or green. Wings held at right angles to the body when at rest. Preys on small flying insects. Larvae develop in water.

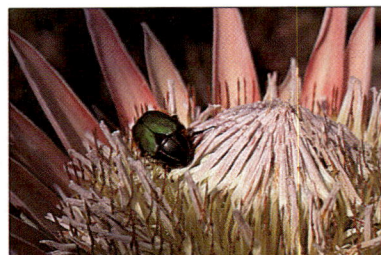

Protea beetles

Small, multi-coloured beetles with strong hind legs. Feed from the flower-heads of proteas, pincushions and other flowers. Inspection of protea blooms often reveals more than one species.

A S SCHOEMAN

Blister beetles

Slender beetles with leathery outer
wings. The back is yellow, red or blue.
Feed by day on flower petals. Body fluids
contain the drug cantharadin which is
capable of causing blisters on skin.

Fruit chafer beetles

Robust, yellow and black beetles which
are unpopular with gardeners as they
feed on leaf buds, flowers and fruit.
They have the unnerving habit of flying
directly at people.

DEON KESTING

Honey bees

Small gregarious bees which feed on
nectar and build honeycombs. Complex
social order, with each colony building a
hive. Barbed sting is left in victim and is
extremely painful; potentially dangerous.

Carpenter bees

Large solitary bees which feed on nectar.
Female bores a tunnel into a plant stem
or soft wood, into which a single large
white egg is deposited onto a specially
prepared bed of pollen. Rarely stings.

Ants

Tiny gregarious insects which are black or
red in colour. Colonies consist of a 'queen',
workers and soldiers. Some species carry
seeds of proteas into their underground
nests – thus protecting them from rodents.

Grasshoppers

Herbivorous insects with powerful hind
legs held in an inverted V-shape above
the cigar-shaped body. Some species are
foul-tasting and gaudily coloured to
warn off predators.

Butterflies and Moths

Butterflies differ from moths in being day-flying and having clubbed (not feathery) antennae. Adults are nectar or sap feeders, and many species drink from puddles or moist soil. Eggs are deposited on the underside of leaves which the larvae (caterpillars) then feed upon; most species have specific food plants.

Watching butterflies is not difficult, but certain techniques will improve your chances of approaching these restless insects. They have good eyesight, so walk slowly towards them, whilst keeping a low profile against the skyline. Avoid casting your shadow over a butterfly, as this is sure to scare it off.

There are several detailed books available, with *Pennington's Butterflies of Southern Africa*, revised by Pringle, Henning and Ball (Struik, 1994) and *Moths of Southern Africa* by Pinhey (Tafelberg, 1975) being the definitive reference works. *Butterflies of Southern Africa – A Field Guide* by Mark Williams (Southern, 1994) is an excellent and easy-to-use guide which features 233 of the more than 800 southern African species.

Garden Acraea
Rust-red butterfly with **partially transparent forewings**. Often seen in gardens. The adults are toxic, and avoided by birds. Eggs are laid on the leaves of Wild Peach *Kiggelaria africana*.

African Monarch
Conspicuous, rust-red butterfly which flies low, in a leisurely fashion. Unpalatable to predators and mimicked by several other species including the female **Common Diadem**.

Painted Lady
Pale orange and black butterfly. The eggs are laid on a wide variety of food plants including the Asteraceae family. Flight is rapid and erratic, but males often pause to display on exposed ground.

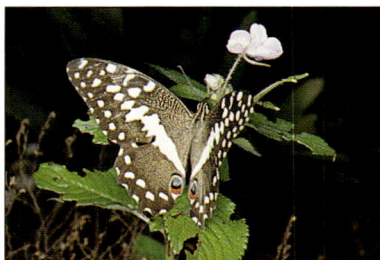

Citrus Swallowtail
Large, yellow and black butterfly with restless flight. Feeds on nectar while beating wings. Males hold territories in bush clumps and gardens. Eggs are laid on plants of the Rutaceae family.

Cape Autumn Widow

Dark brown butterfly with a black blotch on each forewing within which are a pair of blue dots. Abundant in grassy areas between March and May. Flies slowly, just above grass level.

Table Mountain Beauty

Reddish butterfly with orange bands and dots on the wings and a row of small blue spots at the base of each hindwing. Favours mountain tops. Feeds on nectar of red flowers including the Red Disa.

Brownveined White

White butterfly with brown patterns on the wing tips and yellowish underwings. Migrates in large numbers during late summer and autumn. Flies erratically, settling to sip flower nectar.

Common Dotted Border

White butterfly with dark brown spots on the rims of the wings, more prominent in the cream-coloured female. The **underwing is yellow with an orange smear**. Has recently colonised the Peninsula.

Cabbage White *

Large white butterfly with a **single, dark brown spot on the underwing**. Native to Europe, but recently colonised Cape Town, and spreading east. The larvae feed on cabbage and nasturtium leaves.

Heady Maiden

Small, day-flying moth with distinctive **transparent windows in its dark blue wings, and red bands on the abdomen**. Usually occurs in small groups which gather around flowering plants.

Trees and Woody Shrubs

The woody plants of the Cape Peninsula may be divided into four broad categories. Firstly, the varied fynbos shrubs and small trees of which members of the Protea and Erica families dominate. Secondly, the hardy, wind-resistant evergreen bushes such as the Sea Guarri and White Milkwood which grow on dunes close to the shore. Thirdly, the tall trees and bushes of forested kloofs (now greatly reduced in size) including Real Yellowwood and Red Alder. And lastly, the alien trees from other lands (particularly Australia) which have been introduced and now invade many habitats. In addition, numerous species of ornamental trees are cultivated in gardens and parks.

Only the most conspicuous trees of the various habitats are featured on the following pages, with alien species marked with an asterisk (*). Because all of them are common in their specific habitats, it is possible to actively look for the species featured here. Getting to know these common plants will provide you with a solid foundation for further study which, in the case of the great variety within the Protea and Erica families, may require a good deal of dedication. A number of more comprehensive books on the identification of shrubs and trees are available, and the best of these are listed on p. 122.

In this section, the scientific names of the trees are given before the common names. It is important to learn and use these names, as any future study of trees will involve regular comparison between related species and common names are often misleading in this regard; the Wild Peach *Kiggelaria africana* is not, for example, related to the the true Peach *Prunus persica* in any way.

JOHN BURROWS

F

Podocarpus latifolius
Real Yellowwood/Geelhout

Large evergreen tree once common on the eastern slopes of Table Mountain but now rare. Settlers utilised the fine wood extensively for building and furniture, nearly eliminating the species. **Leathery, sickle-shaped leaves held in spirals at the tips of stems**. Large, oval, blue-grey to purple fruits appear on female trees in summer. A fine garden subject.
PODOCARPACEAE Height: 10 to 30 m

M

Widdringtonia nodiflora
Mountain Cypress/Bergsipres

Small, evergreen, conifer tree which grows in groves on east-facing slopes of Table Mountain. Often takes on a gnarled shape. Young leaves thin and needle-like, **mature leaves scale-like, clinging to stems**. Female cone large and woody, silvery-green when young. Vulnerable to fire, but coppices freely. Ideal as an indigenous Christmas tree!
CUPRESSACEAE Height: up to 9 m

Pinus pinea *
Stone Pine

Massive, **open-branched** conifer **native to Mediterranean Europe** but introduced into Cape Town by early settlers. Now a conspicuous element of the landscape, particularly on the lower slopes of Table Mountain. Needle-like leaves in pairs. **Reddish bark is deeply furrowed**. Female cones age to grey; seeds eaten by Grey Squirrel and people.
PINACEAE Height: up to 30 m

M

Pinus pinaster *
Cluster Pine

Large conifer with dense, conical crown. **Native to Mediterranean Europe and North Africa** but introduced into Cape Town by early settlers. Initially planted in a misguided attempt to improve water flow from Table Mountain, now invasive. Needle-like leaves in pairs. **Bark has dark furrows**. Similar *Pinus radiata* has pointed crown and leaves in threes.
PINACEAE Height: up to 15 m

M

Quercus robur *
English Oak

Large to massive deciduous tree **native to Europe and western Asia**. Widely planted by early colonists – some 'giants' are now landmarks in the city of Cape Town. **Leaves oval with rounded lobes**. Small flowers in catkins. Distinctive **acorn held in a scaly cup**. Other invasive, alien oaks in the area include **Pin Oak** *Q.palustris* and **Turkey Oak** *Q.cerris*.
FAGACEAE Height: up to 30 m

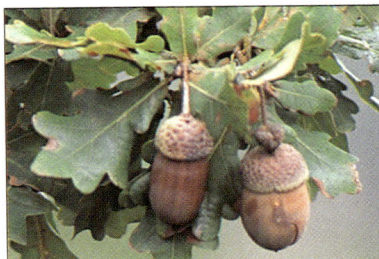

M **GP**

Ficus macrophylla *
Moreton Bay Fig

Large, wide-crowned, evergreen tree **native to Australia.** Planted by settlers; many 'giants' now landmarks in the city of Cape Town. Leaves dark green above and brownish below, with prominent yellow veins. **Trunk buttressed with spreading roots visible above ground**. Ripe figs eaten by birds and fruit bats but seeds not fertile so **non-invasive**.
MORACEAE Height: up to 40 m

GP

99

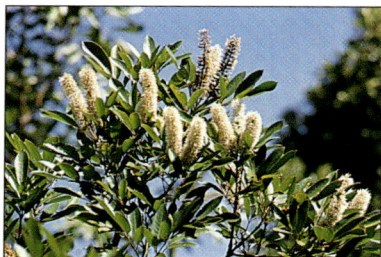

Cunonia capensis
Red Alder/Rooiels

Evergreen tree most common on forest edges and along watercourses. Reaches greatest height in forest but few large specimens remain. Leaves compound with two to five pairs of opposite leaflets and a terminal leaflet; finely toothed. **Stipules are distinctively spoon-shaped**. Flowers are creamy erect spikes from February to May. Fine garden subject.
CUNONIACEAE Height: 5 to 12 m (max. 30 m)

Kiggelaria africana
Wild Peach/Wildeperske

Small to medium-sized tree often found in bush clumps or along streams. Trunk is smooth, becoming rougher with age. Simple leaves are oval, alternate, dull green above, paler and velvety below. Leaf shape is variable, with those on new growth usually serrated. Flowers inconspicuous. **Fruit is a round leathery capsule, splitting to release orange seeds**. Evergreen.
FLACOURTIACEAE Height: 3 to 7 m

Rapanea melanophloeos
Cape Beech/Kaapse Boekenhout

Small to medium-sized tree of forest edges and hillsides. **Leathery leaves** are clustered at the ends of stems; oval, dull-green above, paler below. **Purple leaf stalk is diagnostic**. Small, greenish-white flowers are borne in leaf axils or on leaf scars. Small purple berries clustered on stems. Fine wood used in furniture making, few large specimens remain.
MYRSINACEAE Height: 3 to 6 m (max. 20 m)

Ilex mitis
Cape Holly/Without

Medium-sized tree of forest and forest edges. Glossy, lance-shaped leaves with or without **sparse prickly teeth** on the rim; **midrib sunken on upper surface**, raised beneath. Young leaves and coppice growth serrated. Small white flowers in leaf axils. Small **scarlet berries** produced in abundance from March to July. Lovely garden subject but requires water.
AQUIFOLIACEAE Height: 8 to 20 m

Curtisia dentata
Assegaai Tree/Assegaaiboom

Small to medium-sized tree of forest and forest edges. Wood prized for furniture and bark in demand for medicinal purposes; few large specimens remain. **Opposite leaves shiny green above, pale below with grey or rust-red hairs; margin coarsely serrated**. Small flowers are in sprays. Berries white to red from May to September. Fine garden subject.

CORNACEAE Height: 5 to 15 m (max. 20 m)

Diospyros whyteana
Bladdernut/Swartbas

Bushy evergreen shrub or small tree with drooping shape. Oval leaves are alternate; dark green, shiny and with distinctive soft hairs on margins. Orange or red leaves (dying) may remain on the stems for a while before dropping. Flowers are cream-white bells. Fruits are held in papery capsules, reddish when ripe. Decorative garden subject.

EBENACEAE Height: 1 to 3 m

Rhoicissus tomentosa
Common Forest Grape/Bosdruif

Scrambling, multi-stemmed shrub or climber which reaches into tall forest trees. Leaves large (similar to those of the true grape *Vitis vinifera*, to which it is related), heart-shaped with bluntly toothed margin. **Twining tendrils** are conspicuous. Red to purple berries appear from February to April; relished by birds and people. A vigorous garden subject.

VITACEAE Height: up to 20 m

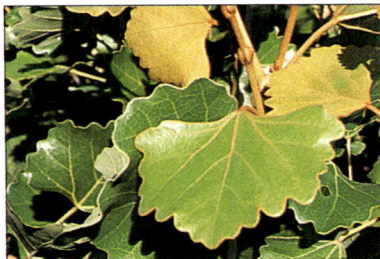

Halleria lucida
Tree Fuchsia/Notsung

Drooping shrub or small tree with rough, flaky bark. Simple leaves are opposite, shiny, finely serrated with pointed tips; bright green, turning purple in autumn. Tubular **orange flowers grow on woody stems and branches**, rich in nectar and loved by sunbirds; appear from May to September. Berries green, ripening to black. Fine garden subject. Deciduous.

SCROPHULARIACEAE Height: 2 to 5 m

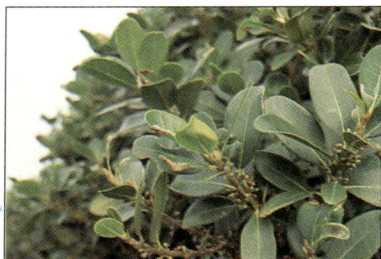

Sideroxylon inerme
White Milkwood/Witmelkhout

Dense **evergreen** shrub or wide-crowned tree of dunes; adapted to withstand coastal winds. Leaves oblong, waxy with pale green midrib; stalk up to 15 mm. Produces **copious milky latex**. Green to purple berries appear from July to January. May reach a great age but large specimens on the Peninsula were lost to early tree-fellers. Fine garden subject.
SAPOTACEAE Height: 4 to 5 m (max. 15 m)

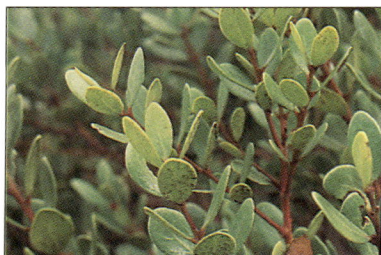

Euclea racemosa
Sea Guarri/Seeghwarrie

Low, dense, **evergreen** shrub of dunes; adapted to withstand coastal winds. Small, oval, leathery leaves resemble those of the previous species but **do not exude milky latex**. Small, creamy-white flowers appear from April to June. Berries are red to purple; appear from July to September. Makes an ideal hedge or screen in sea-facing gardens.
EBENACEAE Height: up to 2 m (max. 4 m)

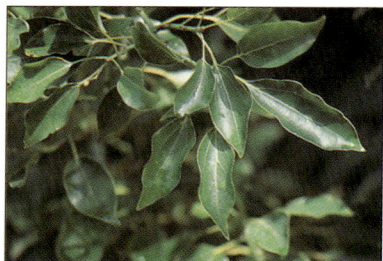

Cussonia thyrsiflora
Coast Cabbage Tree/Kuskiepersol

Evergreen shrub or small tree which grows in scrub on dunes, or at the base of hillsides. Growth restrained by sea winds. Waxy leaves are held in a distinctive, **fan-like arrangement, with five to eight leaflets**. Flowers are borne on short spikes in midsummer; berries ripen to purple from April to June. An interesting garden subject.
EBENACEAE Height: up to 2 m

Cinnamomum camphora *
Camphor Tree

Large to massive **evergreen** tree native to China but for centuries a popular garden subject and brought to the Cape by the early settlers. Leaves pale green, glossy and **fragrant when crushed**. Flowers small, insignificant; in clusters. Black berries appear in autumn. Non-invasive but of historical interest; many giant specimens are now landmarks in the city.
LAURACEAE Height: up to 18 m

Acacia cyclops *
Redeye Wattle/Rooikrans

Shrub or small tree **native to Australia** but brought to South Africa in the 1800s; now a thicket-forming, alien invader of **sand dunes and sand flats**. New leaf growth feathery, but matures into flattened, leaf-like phyllodes (up to 9 cm). **Golden, ball-shaped flowers** peak in midsummer. **Twisted pods** contain **black seeds ringed by a bright red aril**, relished by birds.
MIMOSACEAE Height: up to 6 m

BD SF

Acacia saligna *
Port Jackson Wattle

Willowy shrub or small tree **native to Australia** but brought to South Africa in the 1800s; now a thicket-forming, alien invader of **sand dunes and sand flats**. Flattened phyllodes (up to 20 cm) resemble leaves. **Lemon, ball-shaped flowers** peak in September. **Flat pods constricted between seeds**. Along with *A. cyclops*, it now covers the Cape Flats.
MIMOSACEAE Height: up to 9 m

COLIN PATERSON-JONES

BD SF

Acacia longifolia *
Longleaved Wattle

Willowy shrub or small tree **native to Australia**; now an alien invader along **watercourses and hillsides**. Flattened, leaf-like phyllodes (up to 18 cm); feathery leaves may grow from tips. **Pale yellow, spike-shaped flowers** peak from July to August. **Cylindrical pods constricted between seeds. Brown galls on stems** are a response to predatory wasp larvae.
MIMOSACEAE Height: 3 to 5 m

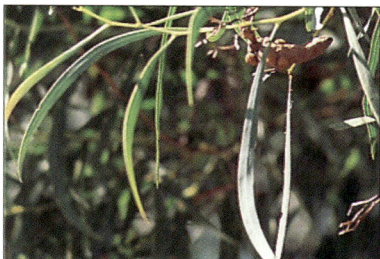

M

Parasesianthes lophantha *
Stinkbean

Scrambling willowy shrub or small tree **native to Australia** but brought to South Africa in the 1800s; now an invader of **stream banks and moist valleys**. **Feathery leaves** bipinnately compound. Pale yellow flowers clustered in small bottle-brush spike; peak in July and August. **Long pods are corrugated, with a small spine on the blunt tip**.
MIMOSACEAE Height: up to 3 m

M WR

Virgilia oroboides
Blossom Tree/Keurboom
Medium-sized tree with sparse foliage, most common on forest fringes and along streams. **Leaves compound** with 5 to 20 pairs of leaflets, plus a terminal leaflet. Flowers **beautiful, lilac, pea-shaped** in clusters; September to March. Flat pods velvety. Bark smooth. Fast-growing but rather short-lived; ideal pioneer species to create a forest clump in a garden.
FABACEAE Height: 6 to 10 m (max. 15 m)

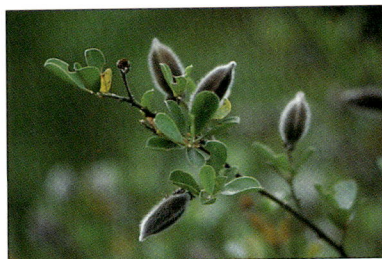

Podalyria calyptrata
Water Blossom Pea/Waterkeurtjie
Bushy, multi-stemmed shrub with greyish-green foliage, most common on forest fringes and along streams. **Leaves simple**, alternate, oval with tip pointed or rounded; leaf stalk swollen. Flowers **showy, pink or mauve, pea-shaped**; solitary or in clusters from July to October. Inflated pods hairy. Fast-growing garden subject but requires plenty of water.
FABACEAE Height: up to 3 m

Sesbania punicea *
Red Sesbania
Slender, multi-stemmed shrub with droopy compound leaves. A **native of South America**, but now an invader of stream banks. Most obvious in summer when the **bright orange, pea-shaped flowers** appear. The pods are distinctive, four-winged capsules. Seeds, leaves and flowers are highly poisonous. Deciduous.
FABACEAE Height: 2 to 4 m

Rhus lucida
Glossy Currant/Blinktaaibos
Dense **evergreen** shrub of sand flats, dunes and lower slopes. **Leaves trifoliate; slightly sticky with a varnished look**, dark green above, paler below. Small flowers in short sprays in leaf axils. Fruit is a small, pale brown capsule; in clusters from July to December. Commonest of numerous *Rhus* species on the Peninsula; all characterised by trifoliate leaves.
ANACARDIACEAE Height: up to 3 m

Eucalyptus lehmannii *
Spider Gum

Medium-sized to tall **evergreen** tree **native to Australia**; now an invader of mountain slopes. Often multi-stemmed; branches may trail close to the ground. Leathery leaves usually **widest near the tip**. Greenish-cream, puffball flowers appear from November to June; the **red buds resemble plastic spiders**. Fruit is a **cluster of spiky woody capsules**.
MYRTACEAE Height: up to 10 m

Eucalyptus gomphocephala *
White Gum/Tuart Gum

Medium-sized to tall **evergreen** tree **native to Australia**; now a vigorous invader of mountain slopes. Elongated, sickle-shaped leaves are **widest near the base**; fragrant when crushed. Puffy cream flowers appear from April to August. The fruit is a small, **bell-shaped, woody capsule** which persists in clusters on the tree throughout the year.
MYRTACEAE Height: up to 10 m

Myoporum tenuifolium *
Australian Manatoka

Dense evergreen shrub or small tree **native to Australia**; now an invader of dunes and sandy areas. **Fleshy leaves** are pointed and **characteristically twirled**; **tiny glandular pores** are visible when held to the light. White flowers appear in clusters from August to October. Small berries are present from October to December.
MYOPORACEAE Height: up to 4 m

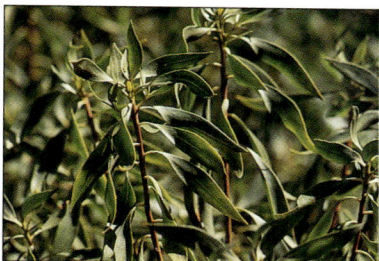

Leptospermum laevigatum *
Australian Myrtle

Dense **evergreen** shrub or small tree **native to Australia**; now an invader of sandy areas. Small, oval leaves are leathery, dull green, with a **small point on the tip**. Bark is furrowed and peels in strips. Small white flowers appear in leaf axils from August to November. Fruit is a **cup-shaped capsule** which may remain on the tree for years.
MYRTACEAE Height: up to 4 m

105

M

Brabejum stellatifolium
Wild Almond/Wilde-amandel
Evergreen shrub or large spreading tree.
Leaves yellow-green, **margin toothed; in
whorls**. Small, sweetly scented flowers in
dense spikes in summer. **Fruit is almond-
shaped, covered in rust-brown hairs**;
appear from April to May. Parts of a
hedge planted by Jan van Riebeeck in
1661 to delineate the Cape Colony are
still alive at Kirstenbosch.
PROTEACEAE Height: up to 8 m

M

Leucadendron argenteum
Silver Tree/Silwerboom
Medium-sized, evergreen tree with **silvery
foliage**; most attractive in summer.
Sexes separate. Restricted to the eastern
slopes of Table Mountain; the finest
groves being above Kirstenbosch and
around Lion's Head. It is fire resistant,
but seemingly rather short-lived. Lovely
garden subject, but the soil around the
stem must not be disturbed.
PROTEACEAE Height: up to 8 m

M

Leucadendron xanthoconus
Sickleleaf Conebush
The most widespread and common of
several similar conebushes on the
Peninsula. A dense evergreen bush with
a **single main stem**. Leaves sickle-shaped
with **fine silvery hairs**. Sexes separate,
female plants bear egg-shaped cones
which persist on the bush. Winged seeds
are released after fire. Similar *L.laureolum*
has broader leaves, and bigger cones.
PROTEACEAE Height: up to 2 m

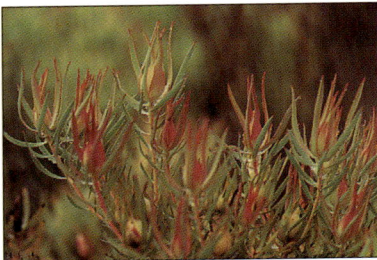

M

Leucadendron salignum
Common Sunshine Conebush
Second most common conebush on the
Peninsula, differing from the previous
species in being **multi-stemmed from
the base**. **Leaves not hairy** at any stage.
Sexes separate, female plants bear egg-
shaped cones with silver hairs. Similar
L.spissifolium is also multi-stemmed but
female cones are hairless.
PROTEACEAE Height: up to 2 m

Leucospermum conocarpodendron
Tree Pincushion/Kreupelhout

Large bushy shrub or small tree with a single main stem, and **leaves with many tips**. Large **yellow flowerheads**, with characteristic protruding styles, attract nectar-seeking Cape Sugarbirds between August and December. Many fine specimens in the Cape of Good Hope N.R., below the Twelve Apostles, and in the Silvermine N.R. Two subspecies occur.

PROTEACEAE Height: up to 5 m

Leucospermum cordifolium
Nodding Pincushion

Small rounded shrub with a single stem and drooping branches. **Not indigenous to the Peninsula** but widely cultivated and conspicuous on hillsides at the Silvermine Nature Reserve and various other localities when spectacular **orange flowerheads** appear during summer; natural distribution is to the east of False Bay to Bredasdorp.

PROTEACEAE Height: up to 1.5 m

Serruria villosa
Golden Spiderhead/Spinnekopbos

Small, heath-like shrub with narrow **leaves dissected and curling upwards** to form a cup around the single **golden flowerheads** which appear in winter. Forms dense colonies. Most common in Cape of Good Hope N.R.; absent north of Constantia. One of several species on the Peninsula: the similar *S.glomerata* has several cream flowerheads per stem.

PROTEACEAE Height: up to 50 cm

COLIN PATERSON-JONES

Hakea sericea *
Sweet Needlebush

Bushy shrub or small tree with **short, needle-like leaves** (up to 4 cm long). **Native to Australia**, it is an aggressive invader of hillsides where it forms impenetrable thickets. Flowers borne in clusters which give the bush a creamy-white appearance. Winged seeds are held in a woody capsule. Closely related *H.gibbosa* has leaves 5 to 8 cm long; *H.suaveolens* has divided leaves.

PROTEACEAE Height: up to 5 m

CAPE NATURE CONSERVATION

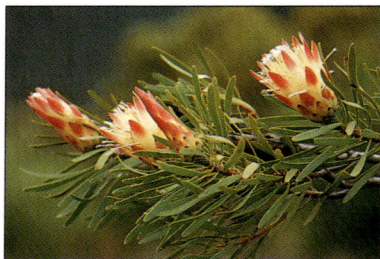

Protea repens
Common Sugarbush/Suikerbos

Shrub or small tree with narrow, blue-green or yellowish-green leaves clustered at the ends of stems. The **flowerhead** never opens very wide, with bracts surrounding the individual flowers varying in colour from cream to pink; sticky to the touch. Flowers mostly in winter and autumn. The seedheads resemble inverted ice cream cones.

PROTEACEAE Height: up to 4 m

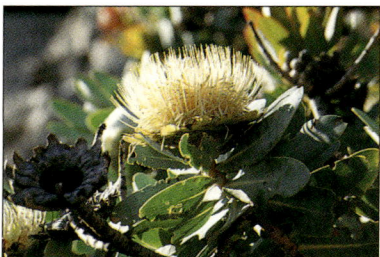

Protea nitida
Wagon Tree/Waboom

Open-branched tree or shrub with broad, blue-green leaves; the **largest of all local proteas**. Large, creamy-white flowerheads appear mostly in midwinter. Most common on the western slopes of Constantiaberg and the foothills of Table Mountain. A local form occurs which may resprout as a multi-stemmed plant from its rootstock after fire.

PROTEACEAE Height: up to 7 m

NICHOLAS COLE

Protea lepidocarpodendron
Blackbearded Sugarbush

Upright shrub with a **single main stem**. Narrow, oblong leaves grey-green, pointing upwards. Flowerheads with pale bracts tipped with **fluffy black 'beards'**. Most common on the False Bay side of the Cape of Good Hope Nature Reserve and western slopes of Constantiaberg. Similar *P.neriifolia*, with white (not black) hairs below the beard, is widely cultivated.

PROTEACEAE Height: 2 to 3 m

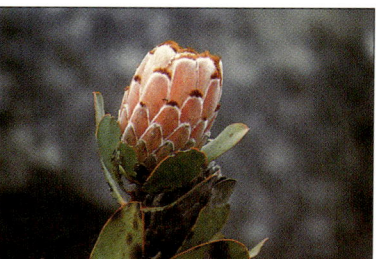

NBI/KIRSTENBOSCH

Protea speciosa
Brownbearded Sugarbush

Upright shrub with **several main stems** arising from a rootstock. Broad oval leaves green with reddish fringe, pointing upwards. Flowerheads with pinkish bracts tipped with **fluffy brown 'beards'**; appear mostly in September/ October. Widespread, but less abundant than the previous species; fairly common on the southern slopes of Table Mountain.

PROTEACEAE Height: up to 1.2 m

Protea cynaroides
King Sugarbush/Koningsuikerbos
Low shrub with **multiple stems** arising from an underground rootstock. **South Africa's national flower**. Magnificent, plate-sized flowerheads vary in colour and shape with pointed outer bracts being rose-pink or creamy-yellow. Leaf shape is also variable but leaves always have distinctive, **long leaf stalks**. Widespread.
PROTEACEAE Height: 0.3 to 1 m (max. 2 m)

Mimetes fimbriifolius
Tree Pagoda/Maanhaarstompie
Small, gnarled evergreen tree with a single stem. Differs from Proteas in having a **large cylindrical flowerhead** with numerous flower-bearing headlets shaded by a **pinkish, cowl-shaped leaf**. Leaves hairy. Endemic to the Peninsula; fine specimens in Cape of Good Hope N.R. and Silvermine N.R. Similar *M.cucullatus* is multi-stemmed with hairless leaves.
PROTEACEAE Height: 2 to 5 m

Mimetes hirtus
Marsh Pagoda/Vleistompie
Dense, much branched shrub with a single stem. Grows in **damp fringes of marshes and along streams**. Differs from previous species by its **bright yellow and red flowers** which appear from May to November. Once common at Newlands and Rondebosch but now confined to Silvermine and Cape of Good Hope nature reserves.
PROTEACEAE Height: up to 2.5 m

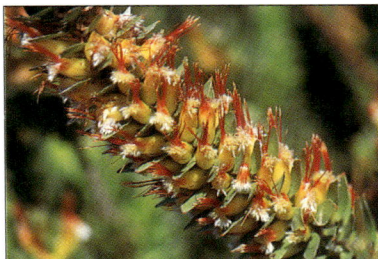

Psoralea pinnata
Fountainbush/Bloukeur
Sparse **willowy shrub** with compound leaves, consisting of small narrow leaflets; clustered on stems. **Pea-shaped flowers are pale or dark blue**, less often mauve; clustered in masses at the ends of stems in early to midsummer. The seedpods are tiny. Almost always occurs alongside running water.
FABACEAE Height: up to 3 m

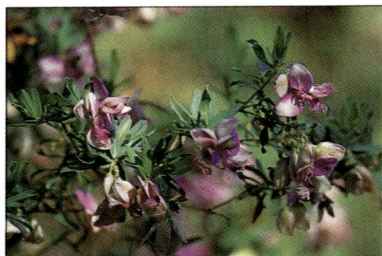

Polygala myrtifolia
September Bush/Septemberbossie
Upright shrub of forest edges, stream banks and dune scrub. Leaves oval, bright green. Pink, pea-shaped flowers appear at any time. Lovely garden plant.
POLYGALACEAE Height: up to 3 m

Liparia splendens
Mountain Dahlia/Geelkoppie
Sparse willowy shrub of mountain slopes and stream banks. Tennis ball-sized flowerheads appear from November to March. Oval leaves have pointed tips.
FABACEAE Height: up to 1.5 m

Cliffortia ruscifolia
Climber's Friend/Steekbos
Small prickly shrub of mountain slopes; may be bushy or sparse. Name owed to its deep root system. Tiny leaves spine-tipped. Separate male and female plants.
ROSACEAE Height: up to 1.5 m

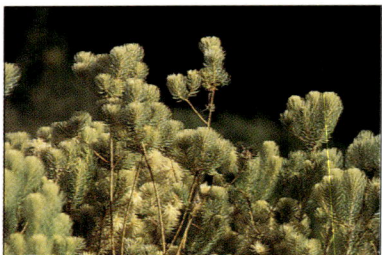

Phylica pubescens
Featherhead/Veerkoppie
Upright shrub of lower eastern slopes of Table Mountain. Narrow hairy leaves clustered on stems. White flowerheads are plume-like. Fine garden subject.
RHAMNACEAE Height: up to 1.2 m

Rubus spp. *
Bramble
Scrambler of disturbed soil along roads and streams; three alien species **native to America and Europe** interbreed. Stems are armed with hooked prickles.
RUBIACEAE Height: up to 1.5 m

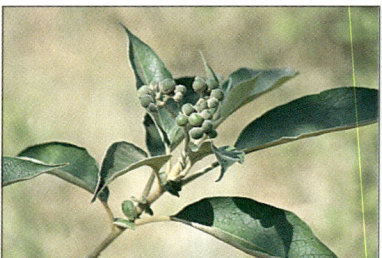

Solanum mauritianum *
Bugweed
Shrub or small tree with slender branches. Leaves oval, pointed, hairy; foul smelling. Flowers lilac, star-shaped. Berries eaten by birds. **Invasive alien** from Trop. America.
SOLANACEAE Height: up to 3 m

Berzelia abrotanoides
Berzelia/Fonteinbos

Low shrub which grows in colonies in moist areas. Slender leaves are crowded along stems. White, ball-shaped flowers appear between August and January.
BRUNIACEAE Height: up to 1.5 m

Hymenolepis parviflora
Coulter Bush/Kouterbos

Low shrub which grows in colonies on hillsides. Soft, needle-like leaves are crowded along stems. Yellow, ball-shaped flowers appear in midsummer.
ASTERACEAE Height: up to 1.3 m

Tarconanthus camphoratus
Wild Camphor Bush/Vaalbos

Shrub or small tree of mountainsides, often close to the shore. Leaves greyish-green above, white below. White, puff-ball flowers from February to July.
ASTERACEAE Height: up to 4 m

Chrysanthemoides monilifera
Bush Tickberry/Bietou

Dense shrub abundant on sand dunes and flats. Leaves fleshy; new growth 'cob-webby'. Yellow daisy flowers appear in winter and autumn. Purple berries.
ASTERACEAE Height: up to 1.5 m

Eriocephalus africanus
Wild Rosemary/Kapokbossie

Small upright shrub of dryer, west-facing hillsides and flats. Tiny leaves fleshy, greyish-green; aromatic. White flowers appear from May to September.
ASTERACEAE Height: up to 1.5 m

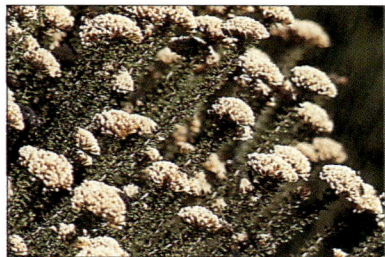

Metalasia muricata
White Bristle Bush/Blombos

Small, much branched shrub of hillsides and flats but absent from mountain tops. **Tiny leaves twisted**. Dense flowerheads appear from April to September.
ASTERACEAE Height: up to 2 m

Adenandra villosa
China Flower Bush

Compact shrublet of mountain slopes; common on the summit of Table Mountain. White flowers have a glossy sheen. Leaves strongly scented.

RUTACEAE Height: up to 1 m

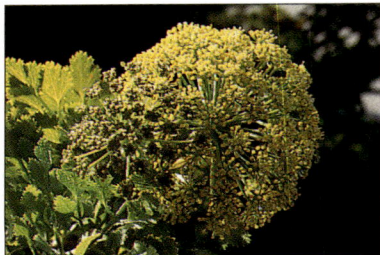

Peucedanum galbanum
Blisterbush/Bergseldery

Sparse branching shrub of upper slopes and summits. Diamond-shaped leaflets serrated. Small flowers in a branched head. **May cause severe skin irritation.**

APIACEAE Height: up to 3 m

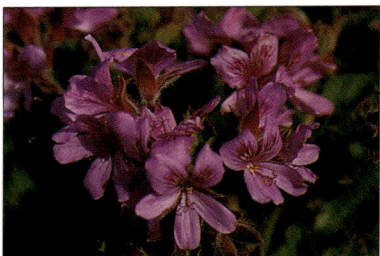

Pelargonium cucullatum
Tree Pelargonium /Wilde Malva

Sturdy shrub of sand flats and lower mountain slopes. Bright green leaves are pleated, hairy and strongly scented. Flowers pink with darker veins; summer.

GERANIACEAE Height: up to 2 m

Pelargonium capitatum
Rose-scented Pelargonium

Low spreading shrub of sandflats and lower slopes. Differs from opposite species in deeply divided leaves and pale pink flowers; Sept. to Nov.

GERANIACEAE Height: up to 50 cm

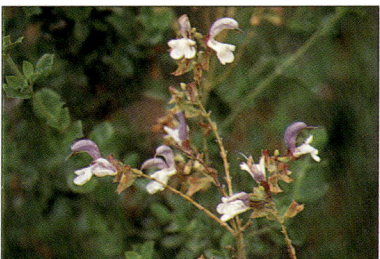

Salvia africana
Blue Wild Sage/Bloublomsalie

Small shrub of hillslopes and sandflats. Distinctive, **blue bonnet-shaped flowers** appear from August to December. Leaves are strongly scented.

LAMIACEAE Height: up to 1 m

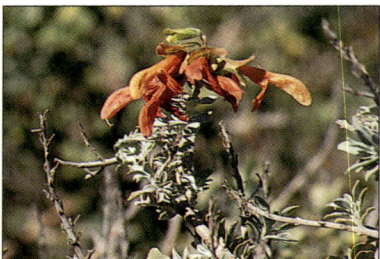

Salvia aurea
Beach Salvia/Bruinsalie

Dense shrub of sand dunes and coastal flats. Hairy, brown, bonnet-shaped flowers appear from June to December. Leaves are greyish-green.

LAMIACEAE Height: up to 2 m

112

Ericas

The Ericas are heath-like plants which, generally speaking, have small leaves clustered along their stems and tube- or bell-shaped flowers. They are amongst the most characteristic of fynbos plants and several of the over 100 species occurring on the Peninsula will be found flowering at any given time.

The identification of Ericas may be rather tricky and requires a degree of specialisation. Just five of the more familiar species to be found on the Peninsula are featured here – for the serious student *Ericas of South Africa* by Schoeman, Kirsten and Oliver (Fernwood, 1992) is recommended.

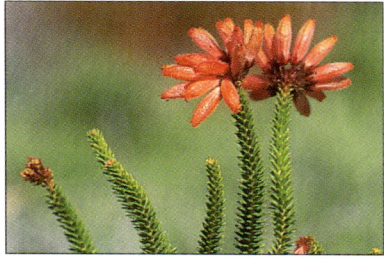

Erica cerinthoides
Fire Heath/Rooihaartjie
Spindly shrub often dwarfed by fire, but resprouts from its rootstock and is among the first plants to bloom after fire. Red tube flowers are hairy and sticky.
ERICACEAE Height: up to 1 m

Erica hirtiflora
Pink Hairy Heath
Bushy shrub of hillsides and marshes where it grows in colonies. Small, **hairy, pink flowers** cover the plant between November and April.
ERICACEAE Height: up to 80 cm

Erica plukenetii
Tassel Heath/Hangertjie
Erect shrub with sparse stems and leaves curling inwards. Flowers with distinctive **projecting anthers** appear from March to September; colour varies greatly.
ERICACEAE Height: up to 60 cm

Erica mammosa
Nine-pin Heath
Slender shrub of sandflats and mountain slopes. **Drooping flowers** appear in clusters from December to May; colour is variable but usually scarlet.
ERICACEAE Height: up to 1 m

Erica coccinea
Red Heath
Bushy shrub of lower hillslopes. **Leaves arranged in tufts up the stems**. Red-yellow flowers appear between April and August.
ERICACEAE Height: up to 1.5 m

Soft-stemmed plants

The fynbos biome supports an incredible variety of small flowering herbs, with geophytic plants (with underground storage organs in the form of bulbs, tubers and corms) being among the most noteworthy. Members of the daisy (Asteraceae), pea (Fabaceae) and orchid (Orchidaceae) families are also well represented.

In this section, only a few of the more conspicuous or interesting plants are featured with representatives from a variety of families. Getting to know these common plants will provide you with a foundation for more detailed study, and may also enable you to place many of the other flowering plants that you are sure to encounter into their genus or family.

There are several books on the smaller flowering plants of the Cape Peninsula, but the flora is so incredibly diverse (over 2 500 species) that no single publication can be regarded as comprehensive. The most useful book is *Wildflowers of the Fairest Cape* by Peter Goldblatt and John Manning (Nat. Botanical Institute, 2000). A list of other useful books appears on page 122.

Haemanthus coccineus
April Fool Lily/Bergajuin
Bulbous plant which produces a scarlet flowerhead **before** its leaves appear; common name refers to those that wait for the bloom to appear after the leaves.
AMARYLLIDACEAE

Nerine sarniensis
Guernsey Lily/Rooi Nerina
Bulbous plant of rocky slopes, only obvious when the striking scarlet blooms appear between March and May. Leaves are narrow, strap-shaped.
AMARYLLIDACEAE

Brunsvigia orientalis
Candelabra/Perdespookbossie
Bulbous plant of sandflats, often close to the shore. Football-sized flowerhead bears red flowers from February to March; when dry it rolls about in the wind.
AMARYLLIDACEAE

Amaryllis belladonna
Belladonna Lily/Maartlelie
Bulbous plant of lower mountain slopes. Thick flower stalk bears a cluster of 2 to 10 trumpet-shaped, pale pink flowers; February to April. Leaves are strap-like.
AMARYLLIDACEAE

BETH PETERSON/AFRICAN IMAGES

114

Watsonia tabularis
Table Mountain Watsonia
Cormous plant of hillsides and moist areas. An erect spike of well-spaced, **salmon-red flowers** appears in **mid-summer**; especially profuse after fire.
IRIDACEAE   Height: up to 1.5 m

Watsonia borbonica
Pyramid Watsonia/Suurkanol
Cormous, clump-forming plant of hillsides. An erect, pyramid-shaped spike of **lilac-pink flowers** appears in **early summer**; especially profuse after fires.
IRIDACEAE   Height: up to 1.5 m

JOHN BURROWS

Babiana disticha
Babiana/Bobbejaantjie
Small cormous plant of north-facing slopes. Leaves are strap-like, **distinctly pleated and hairy**. Lilac flowers appear from July to August.
IRIDACEAE

BETH PETERSON/AFRICAN IMAGES

Gladiolus carneus
Painted Lady/Bergpypie
Small cormous plant of hillsides. Pale **pink flowers, with dark centre**, appear in a spike of 1 to 12 from September to December. Leaves grow mostly at base.
IRIDACEAE

Ixia dubia
Yellow Ixia/Geelkalossie
Small cormous plant of west-facing mountainsides and flats. **Yellow flowers, with orange undersides to the petals**, appear from October to December.
IRIDACEAE

DEON KESTING

Wachendorfia paniculata
Common Wachendorfia/Rooikanol
Small perennial plant of hillsides and sandflats. Pleated leaves are arranged in a fan. Spike of **butter-yellow flowers and brown buds** from July to December.
HAEMODORACEAE

115

Disa uniflora
Red Disa/Rooidisa
Orchid with strap-like leaves. Occurs on the banks of streams and seepages of rocks on top of Table Mountain. Scarlet flowers appear from January to March.
ORCHIDIACEAE

Herschelia spp.
Bonnet orchids
Ground orchids with strap-like leaves. Grow among other vegetation and only obvious when mauve-white flowers appear. Five species occur on the Peninsula.
ORCHIDIACEAE

Cotyledon orbiculata
Pig's Ear/Varkoor
Succulent of dunes and flats. **Leaves are thick, grey-green, rimmed red**. Waxy, dull red, tubular flowers appear on a branched stalk in midsummer.
CRASSULACEAE

Crassula coccinea
Red Crassula/Klipblom
Succulent of rocky hillsides. Leaves are fleshy, hairy-fringed, overlapping on stems. **Scarlet flowers** (rarely white) are in dense heads from January to March.
CRASSULACEAE

Drosera spp.
Sundew/Sonnedou
Small insectivorous plants of seepages and damp places on mountains and flats. Leaves arranged in a fan; **sticky, with red hairs**. Flower borne on a leafless stalk.
DROSERACEAE

Euphorbia caput-medusae
Gorgon's Head/Noordpol
Cushion-like succulent of dunes and lower slopes; **stems sprawl outward**. Contains poisonous latex. Spider-like flowerheads appear in winter.
EUPHORBIACEAE

Leonotis leonurus
Lion Paw/Wildedagga
Bushy shrub which often forms dense stands. Heads of **tubular orange flowers** are irresistible to nectar-seeking sunbirds. Ideal garden subject.

LAMIIACEAE Height: up to 2 m

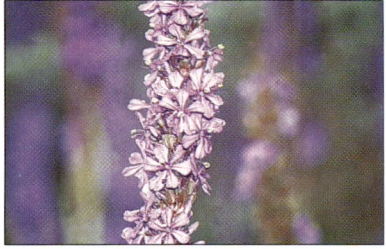

Aristea major
Blue Aristea/Maagbossie
Tall, stiff-leaved, cormous plant of stream banks and damp places on sand-flats. **Dense spikes of blue-mauve flowers** appear in midsummer.

IRIDACEAE Height: up to 1.4 m

Roella ciliata
Lilac Roella
Small spreading plant of mountain slopes. Tiny overlapping leaves are clustered on stems. Distinctive **pale lilac flowers** appear from October to March.

CAMPANULACEAE

Zantedeschia aethiopica
White Arum/Varkblom
Upright plant of marshes and stream banks; distribution aided by people as widely cultivated. **Cone-shaped white flowers** appear mostly in spring.

ARACEAE Height: up to 1 m

Aponogeton distachyos
Cape Pond Weed/Waterblommetjie
Aquatic plant of clear still water; grown in ponds at Kirstenbosch. Broad, **blade-like leaves float on water surface**. White flowerhead is edible; July to September.

APONOGETONACEAE

Harveya squamosa
Brown Harveya/Bruininkblom
Small herb which is parasitic on the roots of other plants. Uncommon but startling when **orange flowerhead** appears during summer. Leafless.

SCROPHULARIACEAE

Orphium frutescens
Candysticks

Small rounded herb of sandflats.
Remarkable only when the **glossy pink
flowers** appear in midsummer. Leaves
are soft and hairy.

GENTIANACEAE

Chironia baccifera
Christmas Berry/Aambeibossie

Small bushy herb of sandflats and lower
slopes. Clusters of **pink flowers** appear
from November to February, followed in
autumn by **small red berries**.

GENTIANACEAE

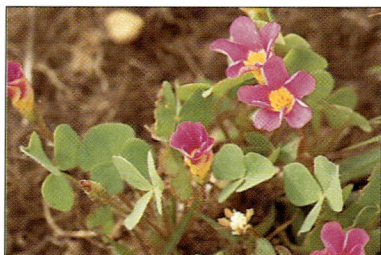

Oxalis spp.
Wild Sorrels

Small, clover-leaved plants with tiny
underground bulbs. **33 similar species**
occur in a variety of habitats. Delicate
flowers may be pink or yellow.

OXALIDACEAE

Lobelia spp.
Wild Lobelias

Small herbs of a variety of habitats. **13
similar species** occur on the Peninsula.
Distinctive, **blue-mauve flowers** appear
throughout the year.

CAMPANULACEAE

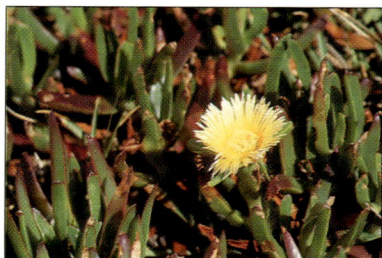

Carpobrotus edulis
Sour Fig/Perdevy

Sprawling, mat-forming **succulent** of
dunes and sandflats; less often on hillsides. **Flowers may be yellow or pink**
and appear mostly in summer.

MESEMBRYANTHEMACEAE

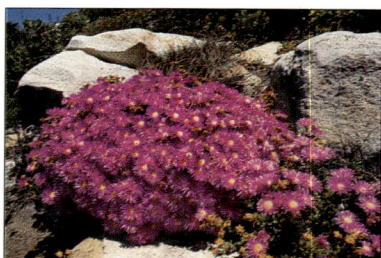

Lampranthus furvus
Purple Vygie

Clump-forming **succulent** of exposed
rocky hillsides. **Shimmering pink
flowers** cover the whole plant in midsummer, closing up at night.

MESEMBRYANTHEMACEAE

Helichrysum vestitum
Snowy Everlasting/Sewejaartjie
Upright bush of hillsides and flats; abundant in Cape Point N.R. **Papery white flowers** appear in midsummer. Woolly leaves are clustered on stems.
ASTERACEAE

Edmondia sesamoides
Yellow Everlasting
Upright, single-stemmed bush of rocky hillsides. **Papery, pale yellow flowers** appear from August to December. Narrow leaves clasp the stem.
ASTERACEAE

Phaenocoma prolifera
Pink Everlasting/Rooisewejaartjie
Upright bush of lower slopes and flats along False Bay coast. **Papery pink flowers** appear from November to April. Tiny leaves are clustered on stems.
ASTERACEAE

Gazania pectinata
Beach Gazania
Low-growing plant of dunes and sand-flats. Flowers may be **yellow or orange, with or without dark blotches** on the petals. Leaves also variable in shape.
ASTERACEAE

Dimorphotheca pluvialis
Cape Daisy/Reënblommetjie
Sprawling or erect annual of sandflats or lower slopes, and along roadsides. **White daisy flowers, with orange centre**, appear in spring.
ASTERACEAE

Arctotheca calendula
Cape Weed
Clump-forming annual of roadsides and disturbed soil. **Pale yellow daisy flowers** may create an impressive display in spring. Leaves are deeply divided.
ASTERACEAE

Restios

Restios are evergreen, reed-like plants with leaves generally reduced to papery leaf-sheaths. The lovely auburn, bronze and fawn hues of hillsides and flats are created by the leaf-sheaths of these plants. The 300 known species are confined to the fynbos biome, with some 100 on the Cape Peninsula. The small flowers are held in spikelets with only the anthers and styles protruding.

Restios of the Fynbos by Els Dorratt Haaksma and Peter Linder (Botanical Society, 2000) describes and illustrates the members of this plant family.

Elegia capensis
Horsetail (Fontein) Reed
Tall, tussock-forming restio with distinctive whorls of soft feathery branchlets at each node on the stem. Grows along streams and alongside marshes.
RESTIONACEAE   Height: up to 2.5 m

Elegia filacea
Bronze Reed
Low, tussock-forming restio with fine green stems. Grows on sandy soils and is abundant at Cape of Good Hope N.R. Bronze inflorescence is at the stem tip.
RESTIONACEAE   Height: up to 50 cm

Chondropetalum mucronatum
Rocket Reed
Tall, tussock-forming restio of damp ground; conspicuous on the summit of Table Mountain. Bronze leaf-sheaths line the stems.
RESTIONACEAE   Height: up to 1.5 m

Thamnochortus lucens
Jackaltail Reed
Medium height, tussock-forming restio. Male plants recognisable by their oblong hanging spikelets. Common on dry gravelly slopes from sea level to 800 metres.
RESTIONACEAE   Height: up to 60 cm

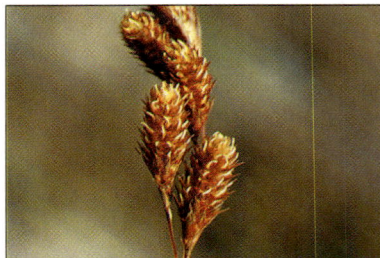

Thamnochortus spicigerus
Olifant's Reed
Tall, robust, tussock-forming restio which grows on sandy soils. Common on Cape Flats. Solitary style protrudes from behind bracts of female spikelet.
RESTIONACEAE   Height: up to 1.5 m

Seaweeds

Seaweeds are not plants in the true sense of the word, but algae. The various forms may be divided into three groups: **green algae** (Chlorophyta), **red algae** (Rhodophyta) and **brown algae** (Phaeophyta). Green algae, which contain the same chlorophyll pigments as land plants, are the most familiar. Seaweeds are most abundant in cooler waters.

The shape of seaweeds varies and includes flat sheets, tubes and fans. Most affix themselves to rocks with a 'foot' or holdfast. No comprehensive guide to seaweeds exists but see p. 122.

Ecklonia maxima
Sea Bamboo/Kelp
Largest of four kelp species in the area. Consists of a **hollow tube topped with strap-like fronds**. Forms underwater forests. Often washed ashore.

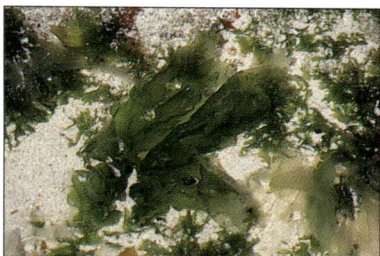

Ulva spp.
Sea Lettuce
Bright green wrinkled sheets attached to rocks by a flat holdfast. Occurs on the edge of intertidal pools and estuaries where it tolerates variable conditions.

Splachnidium rugosum
Dead Man's Fingers
Small, **swollen, yellow-green tubes** filled with a slimy fluid. Occurs on the edge of intertidal pools; shrink when exposed at low tide.

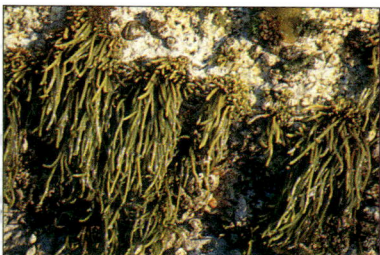

Chaetomorpha robusta
Robust Hair-weed
Rubbery green seaweed consisting of a single row of barrel-shaped cells. Hangs, hair-like, from rocks on the edge of mid- to high-tide pools.

Porphyra capensis
Purple Laver
Rather unattractive slimy sheets attached to rocks in the high tide zone.
Resembles wrinkled plastic sheeting when left dry at high tide. Edible.

REFERENCES AND FURTHER READING

GENERAL

Cowling, R. (ed.) 1992. *The Ecology of Fynbos: Nutrients, Fire and Diversity.* Oxford University Press, Cape Town.

Fraser, M. & McMahon, L. 1994. *Between Two Shores: Flora and Fauna of the Cape of Good Hope.* David Philip, Cape Town.

Hey, D. (ed.) 1994. *The Mountain: An Authoritative Guide to the Table Mountain Chain.* Tafelberg, Cape Town.

Moll, G. 1987. *Table Mountain: A Natural Wonder.* Wildlife Society of S.A., Cape Town.

McMahon, L. & Fraser, M. 1988. *A Fynbos Year.* David Philip, Cape Town.

Paterson-Jones, C. 1991. *Table Mountain Walks.* Struik, Cape Town.

Pauw, A. & Johnson, S. 1999. *Table Mountain: A Natural History.* Fernwood Press, Cape Town.

GEOLOGY

Pritchard, J.M. 1986. *Landscape and Landform in Africa.* Edward Arnold, London.

MAMMALS

Apps, P. 1992. *Wild Ways: Field Guide to the Behaviour of Southern African Mammals.* Southern Books, Halfway House.

Skinner, J.D. & Smithers, R.H.N. 1990. *The Mammals of the Southern African Subregion* (2nd edition). University of Pretoria, Pretoria.

Stuart, C. & T. 1998. *Field Guide to the Mammals of Southern Africa.* Struik, Cape Town.

BIRDS

Chittenden, H. 1992. *Top Birding Spots of Southern Africa.* Southern Books, Halfway House.

Cohen, C. & Spottiswoode, C. 2000. *Essential Birding: Western South Africa.* Struik, Cape Town.

Gibbon, G. 1991. *Southern African Bird Sounds* (set of 6 cassettes). SA Birding cc, Durban.

Ginn, P.J., McIlleron, W.G. & Milstein, P. le S. 1989. *The Complete Book of Southern African Birds.* Struik Winchester, Cape Town.

Hockey, P.A.R., Underhill, L.G., Neatherway, M. & Ryan, P.G. 1989. *Atlas of the Birds of the Southwestern Cape.* Cape Bird Club, Cape Town.

MacLean, G.L. (Ed.) 1993. *Roberts' Birds of Southern Africa* (6th edition). John Voelcker Bird Book Fund, Cape Town.

Newman, K. 1992. *Birds of Southern Africa.* (4th edition). Southern Books, Halfway House.

Peterson, W. & Tripp, M. 1995. *Southern Birds 20: Birds of the Southwestern Cape and Where to Watch Them..* Cape Bird Club, Cape Town.

Sinclair, I., Hayman, P. & Arlott, N. 1993. *Sasol Birds of Southern Africa.* Struik, Cape Town.

REPTILES

Branch, B. 1988. *Field Guide to the Snakes and Other Reptiles of Southern Africa* Struik, Cape Town.

Broadley, D.G. 1983. *Fitzsimons' Snakes of Southern Africa.* Delta Books, Johannesburg.

FROGS

Passmore, N.I. & Carruthers, V.C. 1995. *South African Frogs* (2nd edition). Southern Books, Halfway House & Wits. Univ. Press, Johannesburg.

FRESHWATER FISHES

Skelton, P.H. 1993. *A Complete Guide to the Freshwater Fishes of Southern Africa.* Southern Books, Halfway House.

MARINE FISHES

Branch, G.M., Griffiths, C.L., Branch. M.L. & Beckley, L.E. 1994. *Two Oceans: A Guide to the Marine Life of Southern Africa.* David Philip, Cape Town.

Smith, M.M. & Heemstra, P.C. (eds.) 1988. *Smiths' Sea Fishes.* Southern Books, Halfway House.

Van der Elst, R. 1985. *A Guide to Common Sea Fishes of Southern Africa.* Struik, Cape Town.

MARINE INVERTEBRATES

Branch, G.M., Branch, M.L. & Bannister, A. 1981. *The Living Shores of Southern Africa.* Struik, Cape Town.

Branch, G.M., Griffiths, C.L., Branch, M.L. & Beckley, L.E. 1994. *Two Oceans: A Guide to the Marine Life of Southern Africa.* David Philip, Cape Town.

LAND INVERTEBRATES

Leroy, A. & J. *Spiderwatch in Southern Africa.* Struik, Cape Town

Pringle, E.L.L., Henning, G.A. & Ball, J.B. (eds.) 1994. *Pennington's Butterflies of Southern Africa* (2nd edition). Struik, Cape Town.

Skaife, S.H. (revised by J.A. Ledger) 1979. *African Insect Life.* Struik, Cape Town.

Weaving, A. 2000. *Southern African Insects and their World.* Struik, Cape Town.

Williams, M. 1994. *Butterflies of Southern Africa: A Field Guide.* Southern Books, Halfway House.

PLANTS

Coates Palgrave, K. 1983. *Trees of Southern Africa.* Struik, Cape Town.

Dorrat Haaksma, W. & Linder, H.P. 2000. *Restios of the Fynbos.* Botanical Society, Cape Town.

Goldblatt, P. & Manning, J. 2000. *Wildflowers of the Fairest Cape: Where to Find Them and How to Identify Them.* National Botanical Institute, Cape Town.

Maytham-Kidd, M. 1983. *South African Wildflower Guide 3: Cape Peninsula.* Botanical Society of S.A., Kirstenbosch.

Moll, E. & Scott, L. 1981. *Trees and Shrubs of the Cape Peninsula.* Eco-Lab, Univ. of Cape Town, Rondebosch.

Oliver, I. & T. 2000. *Field Guide to the Ericas of the Cape Peninsula.* National Botanical Institute, Cape Town.

Rebelo, T. 1995. *Proteas: A Field Guide to the Proteas of Southern Africa.* Sasol/Fernwood Press, Cape Town.

WALKING

Lundy, M. 1999. *Mike Lundy's Best Walks in the Cape Peninsula.* Struik, Cape Town.

Rosenthal, G. 1999. *Walking Cape Town.* Struik, Cape Town.

USEFUL CONTACT ADDRESSES

CONSERVATION AGENCIES

Cape Nature Conservation
P/Bag X9086, Cape Town 8000,
South Africa. Tel. (021) 483 4051

**Department Environmental
Affairs and Tourism – Sea
Fisheries** (Media Section).
P/Bag X2, Roggebaai 8012, South
Africa. Tel. (021) 402 3911/3025

National Parks Board of S.A.
P.O. Box 7400, Roggebaai 8012,
South Africa. Tel. (021) 22 2816

NON-GOVERNMENT CONSERVATION BODIES

**Wildlife Society of S.A. –
Western Cape Branch**
P.O. Box 30145, Tokai 7966, South
Africa. Tel. (021) 701 1397/8

WWF - South Africa
P.O. Box 456, Stellenbosch 7599,
South Africa. Tel. (021) 887 2801

**Dolphin Action and
Protection Group**
P.O. Box 22227, Fish Hoek 7974,
South Africa. Tel. (021) 782 5845

OIL SPILLS

S.A.N.C.C.O.B.
P.O. Box 11116, Bloubergrant,
7443, South Africa.
Tel. (021) 557 6155

WASTE AND RECYCLING

The Fairest Cape
P.O. Box 97, Cape Town 8000,
South Africa. Tel. (021) 462 2040

NATURE RESERVES

**Cape of Good Hope Nature
Reserve**
P.O. Box 456, Stellenbosch 7599,
South Africa. Tel. (021) 887 2801

Rondevlei Nature Reserve
Fishermans Walk, Zeekoevlei 7945,
South Africa. Tel. (021) 706 2404

BIRDS

**Cape Bird Club – BirdLife
South Africa**
P.O. Box 5022, Cape Town 8000,
South Africa. Tel. (021) 686 8795

Avian Demography Unit
Dept. Statistical Sciences,
University of Cape Town,
Rondebosch 7700, South Africa.
Tel. (021) 2421/2

Pelagic Birdwatching
Occasional trips organised by Cape
Bird Club (above) or contact
Volante/My Girl Charters
Tel. (021) 783 2906 or
Bluefin Charters (021) 783 1756

**Strandfontein Sewerage
Works** Permits from: Drainage
and Sewerage Branch, 19th floor,
Civic Centre, Cape Town.
Tel. (021) 400 2192

FROGS

Frog Atlas Project
Dept. Statistical Sciences,
University of Cape Town,
Rondebosch 7700, South Africa

FISHES/MARINE LIFE

Two Oceans Aquarium
Victoria & Alfred Waterfront, Cape
Town 8001. Tel. (021) 418 3823

**J.L.B. Smith Institute of
Ichthyology**
P/Bag 1015, Grahamstown 6140,
South Africa. Tel. (0461) 2 7124

Sea Fisheries Institute
(Research Section)
P/Bag X2, Roggebaai 8012, South
Africa. Tel. (021) 402 3911/3025

PLANTS

National Botanical Institute
P/Bag X7, Claremont 7735, South
Africa. Tel. (021) 762 1166

**Kirstenbosch Botanical
Garden**
Rhodes Drive, Newlands. Tel. (021)
762 1166

**Protea Atlas Project
Dept. of Botany – University
of Cape Town**
Rondebosch 7700, South Africa.
Tel. (021) 650 4037

HIKING CLUBS

Mountain Club of S.A.
P.O. Box 164, Cape Town 8000

GENERAL TOURIST INFORMATION

CAPTOUR
P.O. Box 1403, Cape Town 8000,
South Africa. Tel. (021) 418
5202/5214

GLOSSARY OF SCIENTIFIC TERMS

alien – an organism introduced by man and now naturalised in a region or country in which it does not belong

aquatic – living in water

arboreal – living in trees

alternate – leaves which are arranged singly at different points on a stem

anal fin – fin on underside of fish, between pelvic fin and tail

anther – pollen-bearing part of a flower

axil – upper joint between a leaf and a stem

bipinnate – a compound leaf in which the leaflets are further divided into pinna (eg *Acacia*)

bract – leaf-like structure from which a flower arises

compound – a leaf consisting of several leaflets (eg *Virgilia*)

crepuscular – active at twilight, or just before dawn

deciduous – a plant which sheds its leaves at the end of the growing season

detritus - particles of decaying plant or animal matter

dorsal – upper surface of the body

dorsal fin – fin on the back of a fish

drupe – a fleshy, non-splitting fruit

endemic – limited to a particular geographic region

epiphyte – an organism that grows on another but is not parasitic

food chain – the sequence whereby plants are consumed by herbivorous animals which are then preyed upon by other animals

gills – breathing organs of fishes

herbivorous – eating plant matter

indigenous – an organism occur-ring naturally in an area

latex – a white, sticky liquid

leaflet – divided leaf

mimic – one animal resembling the form or colour of another, in order to derive some benefit

naturalised – an organism which has been introduced from elsewhere and is reproducing successfully in a new area

native – *see* indigenous

parasite – an organism which obtains its food from another organism (host)

perennial plant – a plant which lives for at least three years

perennial river – a river which flows throughout the year

petiole – leaf stalk

pinna – divided part of a leaflet

pinnate – a compound leaf divided into leaflets

plankton – small animals or plants which float in sea water

roost - nighttime resting place of birds or bats

simple leaf – an undivided leaf

scale – a thin, plate-like structure

scalloped – leaf margin notched with blunt projections

spike – an elongated stem which bears more than one flower

serrated – margin notched with fine projections

terminal – at the end of a stem

terrestrial – living on the ground

toothed – leaf margin notched with pointed projections

trifoliate – a leaf which is divided into three leaflets

ventral – undersurface

whorled – the arrangement of three or more leaves or flowers at the same point on a stem to form an encircling ring

123

INDEX OF FEATURED SPECIES